HOW TO
IMPROVE YOUR MEMORY

*the text of this book is printed
on 100% recycled paper*

HOW TO
IMPROVE YOUR MEMORY

James D. Weinland, Ph.D.

Professor Emeritus of Business Psychology
New York University

BARNES & NOBLE BOOKS

A DIVISION OF HARPER & ROW, PUBLISHERS

New York, Evanston, San Francisco, London

Manufactured in the United States of America

75 76 77 78 79 80   12 11 10 9 8 7 6

Preface

The roots of this book go back far into the past when, as a young man impressed with the value of a retentive memory, I subscribed to a memory course. Since then my interest in the subject has been sustained through the reading of popular books and articles about memory, study in university courses, and many years of teaching psychology on the college level.

When businessmen and former students urged me to summarize my ideas, I decided to approach the task from the point of view of the professional psychologist. It was necessary to distinguish among hearsay, unproved hypotheses, and objective evidence and to analyze numerous guidebooks and memory systems carefully from the historical, critical standpoint. The resulting volume, which reflects a composite of long-continued interest, training, and experience in this field, should provide a practical, reliable guide to memory improvement.

Many people contributed to the preparation of this book for publication. To all who, because of space limitations, cannot be named here, the author expresses his gratitude. Special mention is due to Miss Rose Bookman and Mrs. Elizabeth Rosebury, who typed the manuscript and provided secretarial assistance; to Professors Rudolph Lagai, Charles Ray, Donald Boell, Arbie Dale, and James Cribbin, of the Management Department of New York University and to Professor Dale Houghton of the Marketing Department, who contributed ideas and illustrative anecdotes; to Professor Arthur Koeppen and Dr. Mildred Marcett, of the English Department of New York University, who read the entire work and improved the presentation; and to Dr. Michael Erdelyi, Industrial Psychologist, who made valuable suggestions.

The manuscript benefited from the expert attention of the publisher's editorial staff, under the direction of Dr. Samuel Smith. Dr. Laurence Hawkins, Consulting Editor, worked on the material far beyond the call of duty, contributing original ideas, emendations, and major revisions.

JAMES D. WEINLAND

Table of Contents

HOW TO
IMPROVE YOUR MEMORY

CHAPTER I

You Can Improve Your Memory

Since you are reading this book, it must be that you are not entirely satisfied with your memory; you may feel that you have a poor memory or that you have a fairly good memory but one that is unreliable and needs improving. If you are a student, you face the necessity of learning and retaining a great many facts, names, dates, and ideas. If you are a businessman or a salesman, you need to remember facts, names, faces, and appointments. The same is true if you are a secretary, teacher, writer, physician, lawyer, engineer, actor, homemaker. . . . In your work and social activities, there are many things you must remember and many more you would like to remember.

But how often you find that you have forgotten to telephone Mr. Brown, you cannot remember Mr. Green's full name and title, you cannot remember the rule about doubling a consonant before *ing*, you cannot recall the author or the title of that book on semantics that you read a year or two ago, and so on.

On the other hand, you are enviously aware that there are people who seem to remember everything. There are, for example, the men, women, and little children who appear on TV quiz programs and amaze us by answering, with apparent ease and confidence, the difficult questions thrown at them. Some of these people give the impression of remembering everything they have ever learned, of being veritable walking encyclopedias. Recently a ten-year-old boy displayed an astounding knowledge of all the physical sciences; a man who described himself as a "laborer" competed successfully with authorities in several fields of knowledge.

1

There are many records of famous historical persons with remarkable memories. Macaulay, at one time, could recite all of *Paradise Lost* without error. William James once memorized the same poem as part of an experiment on memory. Toscanini conducted symphonies without the aid of written scores.

Roscoe Pound, former dean of Harvard Law School, was asked unexpectedly, when traveling in England, to give a series of lectures on legal history. He did not have his lecture notes, but he gave the lectures, with constant citation of laws, cases, and legal opinions, from memory. Comparison between a transcript of his lectures and his original notes showed that he had made only a few minor errors.

General Marshall could discuss from memory almost every event of World War II; he organized and arranged facts in his mind as he did soldiers in the field.

Some people have distinguished themselves—in the annals of psychology, at least—by a remarkable memory for figures. A Dr. Lotte, of Armentières, tells of a young man who could give the cube root of any six-figure number in six seconds. In 45 seconds he gave the sum of the series 1—2—4—8—16, etc., to the 64th power of 2: 18,446,734,073,709,551,615. This "lightning calculator" was blind and an inmate of an asylum for mental defectives —an *idiot savant*.[1] Other *idiots savants* have been able to repeat endless quotations of poetry or repeat with correct pronunciation anything said in a foreign language—although they could *understand* hardly anything said in their own language. Instances of this sort lend support to the popular belief that there is something magical or mysterious about memory and that "you have it or you don't have it."

Some individuals have displayed an exceptional ability to identify people—an ability many of us covet. Napoleon is said to have remembered thousands of his soldiers by name. It has been reported that James A. Farley knew fifty thousand people by their first names. Charles Schwab, when manager of the Homestead Mill, was said to know by name all of his eight thousand employees. Charles W. Eliot, who was for forty years president of Harvard, earned the reputation of knowing all the students by name. Some "memory experts," using association systems, have developed an amazing ability to remember people's faces and names. One of them, Harry Lorayne, can be introduced to hundreds of people, one after the other, and then, facing the same people as an audience, give the name of any person who rises.

At this point you are likely to feel discouraged. All these people, you are no doubt thinking, were endowed by nature with exceptional powers of memory. You probably assume that some people have naturally good, even prodigious, memories and that others (among whom you may classify yourself) have naturally poor memories.

Popular writers on memory improvement tell their readers that there is no such thing as a bad memory, that it is all a matter of training. Such statements cannot be considered entirely correct; they are motivated by the desire to encourage those who lack confidence, who wrongly assume that they "have a poor memory."

For some persons encouragement is essential. There are those who say "I'm a poor speller" or "I'm not good at figures" or "I have a bad memory" and who spell, figure, or remember in a way that is consistent with the idea they have formed of themselves. Such a person can improve his memory only if he changes his concept of himself as one who forgets things. Some people acquire, with time, a perverse pride in their weaknesses and are loathe to correct a fault that has become part of their personality. Having declared "I have a bad memory," such a person feels it necessary to prove it by forgetting things. But being a good forgetter is not a trait to be cherished; it does not contribute to one's success or happiness or charm.

While it is probably true that most people who do not remember well merely need encouragement and training, it would not be realistic to explain excellent memories as entirely the result of training and poor memories as entirely the result of lack of training. For people do vary enormously in every respect. The differences in people's intelligence are not just differences in education. We must recognize the fact of human variation and the fact that one cannot increase his *potential*. A person of normal intelligence cannot become a genius by trying or training. Psychologists agree with William James that effort and training will not improve a person's retentiveness (capacity for remembering), which is believed to be dependent upon the brain structure.

One *can*, however, improve any ability up to the limits of his potential, or capacity. Remembering is a skill like talking, singing, dancing, reading, thinking. Everyone—unless he has some incapacitating defect—can do all these things, but with effort and training he can learn to do any or all of them far better. Skill in reading is a good example. If a group of adults of average intelligence and good education are given twenty hours of suitable training, it can confidently be predicted that they will double their reading speed and improve their comprehension—as a result of learning and practicing certain techniques. Memory training is equally effective. Achieving a better memory is merely a matter of acquiring "know-how."

The same psychologists who deny that training can improve one's *inherited capacity* for remembering say that training can improve the *efficiency* of one's memory. Robert S. Woodworth, in his monumental *Experimental Psychology*, says, of a number of experiments: "All the results obtained in these memory studies are consistent with James's original conclusion that improvement in memory consists in better methods of memorizing."[2] And Woodworth says again, in his *Psychology*, "The process of learning or committing to memory, being a straightforward and controllable activity, is exceedingly susceptible to training."[3] Norman L. Munn, in his *The Fundamentals of Human Psychology*, says of various memory systems that they "facilitate remembering, not by developing some hypothetical entity called 'memory,' as a muscle might be developed by exercise, but by teaching people to utilize various devices which facilitate learning and recall."[4]

In his *Principles of Psychology*, published in 1890, William James reported a rather arduous experiment he had performed upon himself, to test the value of exercising the memory. He learned 158 lines of a long poem (Hugo's *Satyr*) and recorded the time it took him to memorize it. Then he spent a month memorizing *Paradise Lost*. Then he learned the next 158 lines of the *Satyr*, and he found that it took him longer than it did to learn the first 158 lines. He concluded that there was no value in exercising the memory.[5]

But practice in learning brings rewards when it results in mastery of learning techniques and in increased confidence in one's learning ability. Once the United Nations faced a critical situation in which no one could be found to translate an important document into Albanian. A French translator offered to learn Albanian and translate the document into that language if given four days for the job. To the astonishment of the officials he was able to translate the document into Albanian—without error, as was later proved—within the four-day period. This man had already learned twenty languages, and he had acquired "know-how" in the area of learning languages.

Carl I. Hovland, after telling of William James's memorizing experiment in "Human Learning and Retention" (*Handbook of Experimental Psychology*), goes on to say:

> On the other hand, experimenters have uniformly noted the improvement that comes from practice in learning successive lists of the same type. Ebert and Meumann . . . attributed the improvement to better methods of memorizing, discovery of helpful aids, increased confidence, and reduction of anxiety about the learning. . . .
>
> Woodrow . . . reasoned that, if subjects were given systematic instruction in how to memorize, the improvement would be more marked. Accordingly he set up a study with two experimental groups and one control group. One group devoted itself to intensive memorizing of poetry and nonsense syllables. The second group spent the same amount of time but divided it between receiving instruction in good methods of memorizing and performing exercises using these methods. The group that spent all the time in practice performed little better than the control group on subsequent memory tests, but the group given instruction in methods of efficient memorizing showed marked improvement.[6]

This is all rather academic. Let us see how one can remember better in performing an everyday task by using a few simple memory devices. Assume that Mrs. Hausfrau is going to the grocery; she needs steak, milk, cream, frozen peas, carrots, lettuce, and butter. Although she could write the items down and take the list with her, she decides to trust her memory. She could just repeat the list a number of times, and it is not difficult to memorize these items. But suppose that she has acquired a few good memory habits. First she will note that there are seven items; now she will not buy six and walk out thinking that she has finished her shopping. Next she will notice that there are three dairy products, two raw vegetables, a frozen vegetable, and a meat. Next she will visualize herself at the store: she will pick up the three dairy products—milk, cream, butter—first because they are near the door, pick up the frozen peas on the way to the meat counter, and after buying the meat will get the lettuce and carrots. She has now used three common memory devices: numbering, classifying, and visualizing. You might think that she would have done better to write down the items, but through practice Mrs. Hausfrau can do this sort of thing faster than I can explain it or you can read about it.

You can make your memory a much more efficient servant by using these and other devices.

The improvement of memory, however, depends not only on learning new methods but also on motivation. Effective motivation is not just a matter of wanting to improve one's memory but of wanting to remember certain things for certain purposes. Remarkable memories are certainly partially explained by strong motivation. And poor memories are usually to be explained by weak motivation; that is, people are not really very eager to remember the things they complain of forgetting.

Motivation can do wonders. I once interviewed a feeble-minded man who had been committed to an institution because he could not earn a living or function satisfactorily in the community. This man had a remarkable memory in one small area of knowledge. He could tell the day of the week for any date within a period of about twenty-five years. We could trace this ability back to an occasion when, as a boy, he had surprised his teacher by telling her that Lincoln's birthday would come on a Thursday. She praised him, and it was a rare thing for him to be praised for any mental accomplishment. He began to study the calendar, and soon he was able to amaze his classmates with day-and-date stunts. He continued to develop this ability, devoting all his spare time to it. In the institution he was regarded as a mental magician and was given the less unpleasant jobs for that reason. There was nothing miraculous about his ability; it was based on memory developed by intensive and prolonged effort—because his efforts were rewarded.

The memory experts who give public exhibitions of their skill are like this man in one respect—they have devoted all their efforts, over a period of many years, to developing their memories in certain specific areas for the sake of reward. They may have naturally superior memories, but their amazing feats of memory are the product of prolonged, intensive effort, utilizing certain memory devices.

Some people have developed exceptional memories in order to compensate for a handicap. Toscanini memorized musical scores because he had poor eyesight; if he was to be a conductor he had to memorize music because he could not read it while conducting.

Professor Pound developed his ability to remember legal details because of the same handicap. As a law student he had so much trouble with his eyes that he feared blindness, and he determined to make his memory substitute for his eyes.

Charles W. Eliot developed a remarkable memory for people's names and faces because at one time he had been embarrassed by his inability to remember the names of his colleagues and students. Determined to overcome this weakness, he studied ways of improving his memory for names and faces and so finally developed his exceptional ability to identify each Harvard student by name.

It would be safe to say that all persons with remarkable memories developed them because of a driving need or desire. James A. Farley could remember thousands of names and numerous other facts about individuals because he was interested in people and in politics; as a politician he knew that he could influence people more, politically, if he remembered their names and something about their families and interests. Napoleon was able to remember a vast array of military facts because to do so served his ambition.

We all know that there are boys who do poorly in school but, nevertheless, possess an extensive knowledge of baseball. The difference between Bill's knowledge of baseball and his knowledge of spelling is explained by the fact that he is interested in baseball but is not interested in spelling, and also by the fact that his study of baseball is voluntary whereas his study of spelling is imposed upon him.

As a rule, a remarkable memory is remarkable only in one area, the person's career or hobby. But there are some people who have an astonishing memory for things in general. No doubt these people have naturally superior retentiveness; yet we can hardly doubt that they are people who are interested in everything.

CHAPTER II

How Good Is Your Memory—Now?

"I can't remember anything!" Have you ever said this when you were annoyed at yourself for having forgotten something?

However poor you may at times feel your memory to be, you actually remember millions of things. You remember innumerable objects—kinds of objects and individual objects—such as apples, bumblebees, doorknobs, and fingernails, and you know a number of facts about each object (you could easily write a thousand words on what you know about apples). You remember facts about a great many things you have never seen, such as mahogany trees, icebergs, dinosaurs, Pygmies, rickshaws, thyroid glands, and uranium atoms. You may forget a few people, but you remember many people, with their names and a great many facts about them—not only people you have known, but people who lived as long ago as Abraham, and even people, like Tom Sawyer, who existed only in imagination. You have learned many thousands of English words, and, in spite of the erratic and illogical character of English spelling, you remember how to spell nearly all of them. Then, you could, even if you are only eighteen, write a very big book about your life if you tried to remember everything and put it all down. You could write a number of books about your life at this time—what you eat and wear, the house you live in and the other places you frequent, your relatives and friends, what you do for work and pleasure, what you know and think about the world. The amazing thing is not that we forget but that we remember so much.

Yes, you really have a most remarkable memory. Still you are dissatisfied with the performance of your memory in some respects, and that is why you are studying this book.

Perhaps you sometimes expect too much of your memory. You may be annoyed at forgetting something that you never made an effort to remember.

Too many students go through a course making little effort to learn and remember until examination time; then they "cram." Tired and unhappy, they read or skim rapidly through the textbook, hoping to master the contents at one sitting. Such students are giving their memories an impossible task.

No matter how good your memory, it is almost impossible to remember things that do not interest you. If you are a self-centered person, not much interested in other people, you cannot expect to remember the names of all the people you meet. If you are interested in art and not in science, and are taking a course in physics only because you need the science credits, you find it extremely difficult to remember the facts of physics. You can do so only if you develop an interest in the science or if you constantly remind yourself that it is important to you to learn enough about physics to pass the course.

Another impossible task for the memory is to remember something when you are concentrating on something else. The mind is somewhat like a camera: it cannot focus on two things at the same time. If you are taking a close-up of a flower, you cannot at the same time get a sharp picture of the mountain in the background. So you cannot rely on remembering to telephone Mr. D. at ten o'clock about some unimportant matter if you are elbow-deep in work. You can either focus on calling Mr. D. and fail to concentrate on your work, or you can concentrate on your work and rely on a secretary or some automatic device to remind you at ten to make the call.

Many students fail to learn as much in school as they should because they are concentrating so hard on their private desires and fears that they cannot concentrate on what the teacher says.

But you may complain that you forget many things that you are interested in and want to remember. Before you decide that you have a poor memory, put yourself to this test:

What are you most interested in as a hobby—is it a sport, or photography, or jazz records, or stamp collecting, or birds, or gardening, or politics, or science fiction—or something else? You must have a special interest in some kind of activity or knowledge. Whatever it is, do you feel that you have a good or a poor memory for facts in this area? Do you feel that you can or cannot talk intelligently on the subject with others interested in it? Do you feel that if you took a course in the subject you would do well or poorly?

A person is entitled to say that he has a poor memory only if he forgets many things that deeply interest him and that he has made an effort to remember.

Many people are curious to know just how good their memories are in comparison with those of others and would like to take a reliable memory test. There are some excellent reasons why such a test cannot be given in this book. First, the highly validated tests used in clinics cannot be published (if published they would lose their value); they are available only to qualified clinical psychologists. And a test that could be published would not be a validated one; that is, there would be no basis for interpreting the results. Second, the results of a test are affected by the way the test is administered. If the results are to be significant, the test must be properly administered, in a standardized way, by someone who has been trained in psychological testing. Third, you would very likely glance over the test, intentionally or unintentionally, before taking it and, consequently, the results would not be as significant as they would be if someone else gave you the test without your knowing what to expect. Finally, test results should be evaluated in the light of certain facts, such as your age, education, and experience.

It is possible, however, to give some general information about memory testing and to provide some "tests" which may interest you as exercises.

Memory tests must necessarily test immediate recall; for practical reasons people cannot be given material to memorize at one time and be tested on it at some later time. Similarly for practical reasons, a memory test must be short and simple and give easily measurable results.

Memory tests are given clinically as parts of intelligence tests, memory being one of a number of factors in intelligence. For example, in the Wechsler-Bellevue intelligence test, only one of the eleven subtests is primarily a test of memory (immediate recall); but it is also to some extent a test of attention. Memory is involved in other tests—in fact, in all tests—as a minor factor. In a test of general information memory is involved, since one cannot give any information he does not remember.

Memory tests may use either meaningful material or meaningless material such as nonsense syllables or digits. Meaningful material—such as stories, pictures, or sentences—is often used with children, to assure their attention. The objection to meaningful material is that it is more meaningful to some people than to others. With adults, the most commonly used tests employ digits. The tester says that he is going to read some digits and the testee is to repeat them after him—or is to say them in reverse order.

A ten-year-old child of average intelligence can repeat correctly two out of three series of six digits (such as 7-1-8-3-5-4).

A twelve-year-old child of average intelligence can give correctly in reverse order at least one of three series of five digits.

An average adult can repeat correctly two out of three series of seven digits.

A superior adult can repeat correctly a series of eight or more digits and can say in reverse order a series of seven or more digits.

You and another person can test each other's recall for digits in this way. Be sure that both of you understand just what is to be done. Then the person doing the testing should write down a series of digits (not repeating any digit)—six series each of five digits, six series of six digits, six of seven digits, six of eight digits, and six of nine digits. The tester should then ask the other person to repeat after him a series of five digits, saying the digits slowly and distinctly; then the second series of five, and the third series of five—keeping a record of the ones given correctly. Then he should ask the other person to say in reverse order the last three series of five digits. He should follow this procedure with the series of six, seven, eight, and nine digits.

The results should be considered a good test of immediate recall only if the person doing the testing follows directions carefully and if the person being tested is interested, fully attentive, and neither indifferent nor overanxious about the outcome. There should be no feelings of rivalry or hostility between the tester and the testee.

The following is a simple, visual type of memory test which may enable you to compare your memory with that of your rela-

tives or friends who wish to take the test. Of course you will not take the results too seriously, in view of the fact that such factors as interest and motivation can substantially raise or lower your score.

Listed below are forty objects shown in the picture on page 12.* One who is taking the test should locate and point to each of the listed objects and then, without looking at the picture or list again, write down the names of as many of these objects as he can remember. The written list should then be compared with the printed one. One point is scored for each object listed correctly. One who has a superior memory will probably recall most of the objects listed.

1. andirons (in fireplace)	21. knife
2. ashtray (on mantel)	22. lamp
3. ball (in dog's mouth)	23. log
4. bottle (on table)	24. mantel
5. boy	25. mirror
6. chair	26. picture (shown in mirror)
7. cord (window shade pull)	27. pipe (in ashtray)
8. cup	28. plate
9. dog	29. radiator
10. doily (on table)	30. saucer
11. doll	31. skate
12. drape (or curtain)	32. spoon
13. electric fixture (on wall)	33. straw (in bottle)
14. electric light bulbs	34. table
15. electric outlet	35. teddy bear
16. electric plug	36. tray (on table)
17. fireplace	37. tricycle
18. flowers (in vase)	38. vase
19. girl	39. window
20. gun	40. window shade (or blind)

---

* Picture test contributed by Dr. Samuel Smith and used with his permission.

CHAPTER III

The Nature of Memory

If you are to improve your memory, it is desirable for you to understand something about the nature of memory. To begin with, it will clarify things to make certain distinctions and define certain terms.

Memory and Learning. Memory is the foundation of learning; to reverse the statement, all learning is based on memory. The distinctions between learning and remembering are rather arbitrary; there is no sharp dividing line. Perhaps the main distinction is one of time: memory is learning that persists. But the similarity is far more important for us than the difference. All the laws of efficient learning evolved over many years of extensive experimentation are useful guides to the person who would improve his memory.

Memory and Imagination. Memory and imagination both use images from the past. When the images in your memory are true, you have an accurate memory, a replica of something learned or experienced in the past. Imagination is commonly supposed to be the free activity of the mind, creating new things. But, in the final analysis, imagination depends upon memory. You can imagine a flying elephant, a thing that never existed, but the image is just a combination of two well-known things, namely, an elephant and a bird.

On the other hand, what people think they remember is often the product of imagination or of memory combined with imagination. Freud discovered that some of the things people remembered from early childhood never happened. Early in his career, when a neurotic woman told of having been seduced or raped by her

14

father he believed the story, but with more experience he learned that such tales were usually false memories, the product of the desires and fears of childhood. People often take past fantasy for fact, and they often remodel, or embellish (unconsciously) incidents from their past, to make them less humiliating or more flattering to themselves.

Memory and imagination, then, are really sisters under the skin. Imagination is a new combination of memories. And what we call memory is often a mixture of memory and imagination.

Memory and Habit. Both memory and habit are the results of learning. All habits are memories; a memory utilized so frequently that no effort is involved may be called a habit. When we speak of habits we are usually thinking of actions, but there are verbal habits (like saying "Hello" when you answer the telephone) and emotional habits (like getting angry when someone disagrees with you). When you act according to habit, you think only of the present and are unaware that the habit is based on past learning; but when you remember, you consciously return to the past.

Memory, Mind, Intelligence. People sometimes ask, "Is memory a part of the mind?" No, not a part in the sense that the engine is part of an automobile. The mind (as distinguished from brain) is not a physical object, with parts. Memory is a function of the mind, like perceiving and reasoning. The whole mind remembers, but it does other things besides remembering. (Whether a particular memory is located in or associated with a particular part of the brain is another question, to be touched on later.)

Memory and intelligence are integrated, since all intelligence is based on memory, and intelligence has often been defined as "ability to learn." Widely used intelligence tests, like the Stanford-Binet and the Wechsler-Bellevue tests, contain subtests that are purely memory tests, and memory is necessarily involved in all tests. As a rule, the more intelligent the person, the better his memory, but, since intelligence is more than memory, the correlation is not high. Some low-grade mental defectives have had wonderful powers of rote memory, being able to memorize a great deal without effort, while understanding nothing.

Retention, Recall, Recognition. These terms are much used in scholarly writing about memory. *Retention* is synonomous with memory in the sense of capacity for remembering. Retention is "potential recall," the holding of something in the mind, which may possibly be recalled at some later time. *Recall* means bringing a memory to consciousness; it is a particular instance, or evidence, of retention. As you well know, you cannot recall, at any one moment, everything you retain in your memory. You have had the experience of trying unsuccessfully to recall something, which pops into your mind at a later time when you are not trying to recall it. Recall is like a spotlight thrown into the darkness of the vast storehouse of memory; it can illuminate only one thing at a time, and, though the light is played here and there constantly, it may not fall upon a particular memory for many years, perhaps never. It may be said that recall is the spotlight, retention the storehouse.

Recall may be voluntary, as when you search for a fact that you have learned, or it may be involuntary, as when a fact comes into your consciousness without being invited.

Recognition as a technical term means just what it means in everyday usage. The difference between recall and recognition can be illustrated by two types of tests. If I were to test you on the contents of Chapter I, I might ask: "What persons were mentioned who had unusual memories for people's names?" Or "What does motivation have to do with memory?" This would be a test of recall. But I might ask: "Who had a remarkable memory for legal matters: (a) William James? (b) Eliot? (c) Pound? (d) Farley? (e) Dr. Lotte?" Or: "Toscanini had a remarkable ability to memorize poetry. True or false?" This would be a test of recognition. Tests based on recognition (multiple-choice and true-or-false tests) are easier than tests based on recall, because we can recognize more than we can recall. Recall and recognition are two kinds of remembering, the former active, the latter passive.

Reminiscence. This word is given a special meaning by psychologists: it refers to the fact that memory for a subject incompletely learned is generally better two or three days later than at the time practice was completed.

Now, after all these distinctions, we are ready for the question, What is memory? This is a question like, What is energy? and the answer is simple: Nobody knows. But we do know a great many facts about memory.

The Association of Ideas. So far as we know, Plato was the first man to give thought to the nature of memory. Plato, a mystical philosopher and not a scientist, believed that all knowledge is recollection, the imperfect remembering of some of the perfect knowledge possessed by the soul in its previous incorporeal existence. This notion we regard as unfounded and useless. But Plato arrived at another notion, based on observation of his own mind, that is still valid and that has been and is tremendously useful. He pointed out the fact that ideas are connected, or related, by associations.

In Plato's dialogue entitled *Phaedo,* Socrates says that although a lyre is something very different from a man, yet one who sees only the lyre may form an image of the man who owns and plays it. And one who sees Simmias may recall his friend Cebes, "and there are endless examples of the same thing." "When we perceive something . . . from that perception we are able to obtain a notion of some other thing like or unlike which is associated with it but has been forgotten."[1]

That is, all ideas are associated with other ideas. No thoughts stand alone and isolated in the mind. Like people, ideas belong to families, tribes, nations.

Aristotle, a great classifier, distinguished four kinds of association: (1) spatial contiguity (thumb and fingers), (2) temporal contiguity (World War II and the atomic bomb), (3) similarity (horse and cow), (4) contrast (black and white). We could think of others—for example, cause and effect (fire and heat), part and whole (nose and face), particular and general (bee and insect), numerical contiguity (five and six).

St. Augustine pointed out that ideas become associated only by experience (which was implied by Plato), and he reduced Aristotle's four kinds of association to coexistence—that is, to ideas that have been active together in the mind at the same time. This insight remains valid for modern psychologists, who regard contiguity of experience as the basic factor in association.

Pavlov, the discoverer of what we now call *conditioning,* showed how association through experience can link unlike things. In a famous experiment he rang a bell each time he offered food to a hungry dog; after about twenty such experiences the dog salivated when he heard the bell even though no food was offered. There is no similarity between food and the sound of a bell; the association is an example of association by contiguity of experience. The behaviorist school of psychology derives from Pavlov's experiments on conditioning.

The association of ideas concept has been given various interpretations by philosophers and psychologists, but it remains an important foundation stone of psychology and is widely used today—in psychological tests, psychoanalysis (free association), lie detectors, and certain memory systems.

Can we derive anything of practical value from an awareness of the association of ideas? William James says:

> The more other facts a fact is associated with in the mind, the better possession of it our memory retains. Each of its associates becomes a hook to which it hangs, a means to fish it up by when sunk beneath the surface. Together they form a network of attachments by which it is woven into the entire tissue of our thought. The secret of a good memory is thus the secret of forming diverse and multiple associations with every fact we care to retain.[2]

A conscious use of this principle was made by the historian Gibbon. Before setting to work on a new historical subject, he would sit alone or take a long walk and bring to mind everything he already knew on the subject. With this associational complex fresh and ready for new associations, he would then go to work.

Memory is in one respect like money. The more money one has, the more interest it earns, which increases the capital and earns still more money. The more memories one accumulates, the more easily new memories are accumulated, which increase one's memory capital and earn more memory interest. Memories breed memories.

Memory and the Brain. The basic theoretical problem of psychology—which may be insoluble—is that of the relation between mind and brain. This is, of course, not a practical problem as regards memory improvement. But it deserves at least a glance here.

Primitive man believed that the mind is a spirit independent of the body. Dreams led him to believe that when the body is asleep the mind goes wandering freely, and he came to believe that when the body dies this spirit lives on without the body.

For us, in this more or less scientific age, the question remains, how can the mind, which is immaterial, be lodged in a biochemical substance such as the human brain? No one can answer this question precisely although we do know that ideas and brain cells are associated in some way. We do not believe that the brain is the mind, but that the mind is somehow dependent upon the brain.

It was observed even in antiquity and in the Middle Ages (as by St. Thomas Aquinas) that injuries to the brain sometimes damage the memory and personality, and this has come to be a matter of common popular knowledge. We also know that when blood leaves the brain temporarily, as in a faint, consciousness disappears. And consciousness likewise disappears when bodily energy is at a minimum, in deep, dreamless sleep.

As a result of modern knowledge of brain structure and experimentation, the belief is generally accepted by psychologists that everything experienced or learned produces some physical change in the brain, leaves a trace of some kind. The trace, whatever it may be, is sometimes called an *engram* (something "written on" the brain).

The question is, where and what is the memory when it is not present in consciousness? Suppose a man of fifty is being psychoanalyzed and is making an intensive effort to dredge up memories from his early childhood. As he recalls early memories, these bring up others attached to them. Now he suddenly remembers being frightened by a big black dog when he was two or three. He has not thought of the incident for almost fifty years. Where has the memory of the dog been all that time?

Microscopic examination of the nervous system (which includes the brain) shows it to be composed of billions of cells (of various shapes according to their function) called *neurons*. Each neuron has on one side a long fiber ending in a brush, called the *axon*, and on the opposite side a number of highly branched short fibers called *dendrites*. The place of contact between the axon of one cell and the dendrites of another is called the *synapse*. This communication system is the physical basis of the association of ideas. The memory "trace" spoken of earlier may be a lowering of the resistance to passage of the nervous impulse from one cell to another, so that the next impulse passes across more easily. It is still, of course, extremely mysterious how an electrochemical impulse passing through a number of cells in this way can create in the mind a picture of a dog and the sound of the dog's barking.

Whether a specific datum of memory is localized in a particular cell or group of cells is an unanswered and controversial question.

Support for the localization theory has come from the recent discovery that vivid memories are created if the cerebral cortex is touched with an electric needle (when a portion of the skull has been removed in the course of a brain operation). Dr. Wilder Penfield, director of the Montreal Neurological Institute, reports that one girl thus treated heard familiar music so clearly that at first she believed that a phonograph had been turned on nearby. A man said that he heard his cousins talking and laughing, although he knew that they were far away. According to Dr. Penfield the nervous system retains a complete record of a person's past that is like "a continuous strip of movie film, complete with sound track."[3]

The psychologists Morrow and Cohen gave a number of memory tests to forty-four brain-damaged war veterans and found them deficient in all kinds of recall except for old visual material.[4]

Another psychologist, Brickner, reported his careful observation of a stockbroker whose frontal lobes had been removed. Although the man continued his work for some time, his memory for recent events was poor, he was incapable of abstract thinking, and he became emotionally unstable, deficient in self-criticism and self-control. His memories of his childhood and youth were not affected.[5]

Clifford T. Morgan, writing on "Localization of Memory Functions in the Brain" in the Handbook of Experimental Psychology (1951), says: "There is a vast literature concerning memory losses in human beings suffering lesions of the brain. As one might expect, most of the studies were conducted under clinical conditions in which it is hard to get either adequate tests of the psychological deficit or precise data on the parts of the brain affected."[6] There has been much experimentation on animals. From studies of monkeys whose prefrontal lobes have been removed or severed, only one clear conclusion can be drawn: that in such monkeys the power of attention is weakened. Morgan concludes: "Here let us simply note that there is no simple localization of particular memories in different areas of the brain. We may eventually find, however, that factors are localized in particular areas but that each factor is involved in several kinds of memory."[7]

For our purposes we may define the memory as the whole mind working to bring back information from the past.

Thorndike's Laws of Learning. Edward E. Thorndike, who began his psychological career by making cats and chickens memorize for their meals and who later extended his observations and experiments to college students, formulated certain laws of learning. Among them were the laws of "readiness," "frequency" ("exercise"), and "effect."

The "law of readiness" is merely a statement of the importance of motivation. Readiness is preparation for action. With Thorndike's experimental animals it was a matter of hunger; a cat that wanted to get out of its cage to be fed was ready to learn how to do so; it did many things at random and finally performed the action that opened the door. Of course the principle of readiness applies to human beings. A schoolboy supposed to study arithmetic at two o'clock may be anticipating getting out of school and being free to play at three. His readiness is for play and he has no readiness for learning arithmetic. On the other hand, if he likes singing and the teacher says, "Today we are going to learn a new song," he will be in a state of readiness to learn the song.

The "law of frequency" was based on the fact that when the cat performed the act that opened the door of its cage, it apparently made no association between what it had done and the result. But after a number of trials it did make the association and learned to do the right thing immediately. The principle, applied to human learning, is expressed in the saying "Practice makes perfect." But frequency of repetition produces results only if readiness accompanies it, as parents and teachers know by experience. The law of frequency, or exercise, does not apply to all learning. A striking fact, such as something that contradicts one's beliefs or provides new insight, may be learned once and for all time. When a child learns that the world is round, he is amazed and impressed and does not have to be told that it is round again and again, as he does with such a fact as $6 \times 7 = 42$.

Thorndike derived his "law of effect" also from his experiments with animals; they learned because learning brought a reward: food. The law of effect certainly applies to a great deal of human learning. A person may learn something just because it brings him a feeling of satisfaction. But more often, perhaps, people learn for the sake of a reward from others. Children and older students often study for the sake of getting good grades and pleasing their parents and teachers. High-school students may study in order to be able to go to college, and college students in order to graduate—for the sake of prestige and more earning power. Business and professional people study for the sake of a better job, bigger salary, more prestige.

It has been objected to the law of effect that people sometimes learn, not to win a reward, but to avoid punishment; however, the concept of reward might be stretched to include avoidance of punishment.

Thorndike believed that the law of effect would cause people to remember pleasant things and to forget unpleasant things. Something will be said about this question in the next chapter.

Thorndike later announced the "law of belongingness," which was his way of saying that meaningful associations are more easily remembered than meaningless associations. True. It is easier to learn "Psychology is a very interesting science" than "Geography by a wavy intimidate essence," which, in turn, is easier than "Effolovy ab u nory insimmading vellence." J. P. Guilford reported an experiment in which a group memorized 15 nonsense syllables, 15 unrelated words, and 15 related words. The group required, on the average, 3.5 trials to learn related words, 8.1 trials to learn unrelated words, and 20.4 trials to learn nonsense syllables.[8]

The Importance of Pattern (Gestalt). One of the basic scientific impulses is to take things apart to see what they are made of and what makes them tick (analysis). As a result of this preoccupation, scientists have concentrated on parts and have tended to neglect wholes. A reaction against "psychological atomism" produced the German school of Gestalt (the word is variously translated as "form," "configuration," or "pattern"). It stresses the importance, in perception, learning, memory, and thinking, of the whole, which Gestalt psychologists say is more than the sum of its parts.

The way we think in terms of wholes can be easily illustrated: Look at the following letters: n v th l s. It is probable that you recognize the word nevertheless in spite of the omission of six of the letters. If you did not have a tendency to form things perceived into familiar patterns, you would see only six spaced and meaningless letters.

The bearing of this way of thinking upon memory is this: We

learn and remember not only by associating one thing with another but also by combining many things into a pattern, or meaningful whole. In studying a body of knowledge, invest most of your effort in learning the outlines of the subject, the framework, and then fit into this framework, in their proper location, as many details as you can.

Unfortunately, the Gestalt principle leads to error as well as learning. If you come upon the word *adsorb*, it is very likely that, if you are not a chemist or a student of chemistry, you will see it as *absorb*, a much commoner word. Spelling errors are partly due to people's tendency to see the whole word as a shape and not to notice the separate letters. Editing copy and proofreading require a special ability and special effort because we tend to see the letters we expect instead of the ones that are actually on the printed page.

People's memories are distorted by their preference for familiar patterns. A group of students was shown a set of pictures, one of them a picture of a Negro and a white man, the latter with a razor in his hand, facing each other in menacing attitudes. Later, when a number of the students were asked to recall the picture, they "remembered" the razor as being in the Negro's hand.[9]

In abnormal psychology there is a formulation called "Hodgson's law," which states that we often remember a thing in the way we want to remember it. We twist or modify it until it pleases us. Once the material has been changed to satisfy us emotionally, it tends to remain in that form.

F. C. Bartlett conducted an interesting experiment which throws light on patterned remembering.[10] He asked one person to read a passage, then to retell it to another person, asked this person to relay it to a third, and so on. Here is one of the selections he used:

The Intellect Is Vagabond

Traveling is a fool's paradise. We owe to our first journeys the discovery that place is nothing. At home, I dream that at Naples, at Rome, I can be intoxicated with beauty, and lose my sadness. I pack my trunk, embrace my friends, embark on the sea, and at last wake up in Naples, and there beside me is the stern Fact, the sad Self, unrelenting, identical, that I fled from. I see the Vatican and the palaces. I affect to be intoxicated with sights and suggestions, but I am not intoxicated. My giant goes with me wherever I go.

But the rage for traveling is only a symptom of a deeper unsoundness affecting the whole intellectual action. The intellect is vagabond, and the universal system of education fosters restlessness. Our minds travel when our bodies are forced to stay at home. We imitate, and what is imitation but a traveling of the mind?

At the fifth retelling, this had been reduced to the following (and at the tenth retelling it was essentially the same):

Traveling is a very good thing for people who are in sorrow or trouble. Being in trouble myself, I determined to travel. I first went to Naples, but that beautiful town had no effect upon me. I went to Rome, but even that place made no difference to me, so I returned home with my troubles.

The most noticeable change is a reduction in length, which was largely the result of the hearer's being unable to remember all of the story as told to him. The next most noticeable change is that the literary language of the original was translated into simple, commonplace language.

But if we carefully compare the original and the fifth version we discover that the transformation is not merely one of reducing and simplifying. The thought was distorted in the process of passing from one person to another. The original began, "Traveling is a fool's paradise." The first two tellers retained this beginning. The third kept the idea but changed the wording: "Traveling is ridiculous if intended to make one forget one's self and one's troubles"; however, he concluded with "Traveling is a fool's paradise as [i.e., if] viewed as a means of forgetfulness." Note that this person qualified the author's statement "Traveling is a fool's paradise." The fourth teller dropped the "fool's paradise" altogether (though it is a striking phrase) and began "Traveling has often been used as a means to make us forget ourselves and our troubles." And then the fifth person said: "Traveling is a very good thing for people who are in sorrow or trouble." Narrators 6 to 10 reduced this to "Traveling is good for people in trouble." The author's opening statement was turned into its opposite. Why? Because people generally want to travel and regard traveling as a fine thing. To say that traveling is a fool's paradise contradicts the common opinion and implies that the person who wants to travel is a fool. So the third teller softened the statement, making it less absolute; the fourth ditched "fool's paradise" and made a rather noncommittal statement that "Traveling has often been used to make us forget . . . our troubles." The fifth person strengthened the statement, saying that "Traveling is a very good thing," etc. This statement was acceptable to subsequent narrators and so went unchanged. In the fifth and subsequent tellings the first sentence is contradicted by what follows.

Another striking change occurred. The ideas contained in the second paragraph of the original disappeared, although it is clear that for the author these thoughts were more important than those in the first paragraph. (And we usually remember best what comes at the end of something read or heard.) The first teller simplified and softened the second paragraph to: "Traveling is a symptom of the restlessness that comes from education. We are always moving, for even when our bodies are at home, our minds are traveling far abroad." The second teller said almost the same thing. The third dropped the thought entirely. The reason the thought of the second paragraph was not transmitted was that it was unfamiliar, incomprehensible, and rather forbidding.

So when we remember something complicated, we simplify it (which is necessary), forget details and things we cannot understand, and too often distort the thing to fit the familiar patterns of our minds.

It has often been stated that there is no organization or pattern to the world except that which the mind puts there. Everyone organizes his own private world and remembers best the items that fit into the pattern. The artist sees the world in terms of form and color; the physician sees it as inhabited by bodies having various diseases and ailments. The paranoic organizes his world around himself and his enemies.

CHAPTER IV

Why We Forget

In order to understand memory we also have to understand forgetting, the "tails" side of the memory coin.

People often want to forget. In this book, however, we discuss forgetting in its negative aspect—as something undesirable, as an obstacle to be overcome. But, for the sake of fuller understanding, we shall consider both active (purposeful) forgetting and passive (undesired) forgetting.

"Forgetting" Sometimes Incomplete Learning. We sometimes think we have forgotten something when the fact is that we have never learned it or have not learned it well. If something is to be retained in the memory, subject to recall, it must be correctly, clearly, and forcibly impressed on the mind at least once. Incomplete learning is usually due to lack of attention arising from lack of interest or the interference of other matters.

Thus, if you say, "I've forgotten that man's name" or some other item, it is possible that you never gave it your attention in the first place.

Forgetting Usually a Matter of Recall, Not Retention. Some psychologists have believed that, as regards retention, if there is no brain injury or atrophy, nothing is ever forgotten; that is, a memory trace once made on the nervous system remains permanently. This belief is contrary to the common opinion that forgetting is due to fading, as if memories were written in an ink that gradually fades until it is illegible, or were like a path through a grassy meadow which if not used grows over again and disappears.

The statement that nothing experienced is ever completely forgotten is incapable of proof, but there is some evidence that it may be true.

Would you believe that a child under three years of age, of English-speaking parents, would retain for years the memory of selections from ancient Greek that were read to him at that early age? The psycholoigist H. E. Burtt proved the fact with his own child. When the boy was fifteen months old, Burtt began to read him daily three selections from Greek literature. He continued this practice until the boy was three years old, reading the same three selections daily for three months, then three new selections for three months, and so on. (The child did not learn Greek as a language; he never knew the meaning of what was read.) At the age of eight and a half, the boy memorized a third of these selections and some new selections from the Greek. He learned the selections that had been read to him six or seven years earlier in 70 per cent of the time required for an equal amount of new material. (This is the "savings" method of testing retention.) At the age of fourteen, a similar test was made, and a saving of 8 per cent was found. A final test was made at eighteen; this time there was no evidence of retention. This experiment obviously does not prove that "nothing is ever forgotten," but it proves that there is more retention than we would expect.[1]

There are even more striking evidences of retention than Burtt's experiment. A classical instance of amazing retention is the following: A German woman in a trance state began to speak in a strange tongue, which was finally identified as Hebrew. She had never learned or studied Hebrew. But many years before, she had been a servant in the home of a Hebrew scholar, who had sometimes in her hearing spoken Hebrew or read it aloud.[2]

As mentioned in the preceding chapter, Dr. Penfield's experiments with the electric needle stimulating the exposed cerebral cortex led him to declare that the nervous system contains a complete record of the person's past.

Present-day psychotherapy uses various means of recovering "forgotten" memories, especially those of early childhood when the patient's neurosis was being formed. There is nothing mysterious about the method of psychoanalysis. The analyst encourages the patient to recall as much as possible about his childhood. As the patient dwells on his childhood, one memory leads to another associated memory. At first the patient consciously conceals many of his experiences and thoughts because he considers them shameful. But if the analyst is able to convince the patient that he is tolerant and understanding and sympathetic, the patient will reveal more and more of this "secret" material and will finally be able to recall many things he had repressed (pushed out of consciousness) because they were humiliating and frightening. Defensive forgetting will be discussed at greater length later; the point at present is that through psychoanalysis old, "forgotten" memories are recalled.

Recently there has been a renewed interest in hypnosis (long rejected by psychoanalysts) because it provides easier and quicker access to repressed memories than the slow process of psycho-analysis. When a hypnotized subject recalls an old, painful experience and then, when awake, recognizes and acknowledges the memory as an authentic recollection of his past (which he is sometimes unable or unwilling to do), recovery from his neurosis usually comes quickly. Here is a typical recall of a "forgotten" experience, reported by Morton Prince. The patient, a woman of about forty, told him while in a hypnotic trance:

I was eight years of age, and we were at Bar Harbor for the summer. There was a noisy brook there coming down from the hills. It was called Duck Brook. The older girls used to go there and go walking with the boys. One Sunday I went there with my governess. A boy was with us. But in a short while, the boy left and went off looking for the other girls. I was very sad because I felt that life would always be like that; that I was ugly and unattractive, and my friends would always leave me for someone else. All the rest of the summer I refused to go to any parties, and everyone thought I was sullen.[3]

Some of the most amazing revivals of apparently dead memories occur through the hypnotherapist's use of the technique of "re-gressing" a patient. As Dr. Clara Thompson says, in her book *Psychoanalysis: Evolution and Development*: "When this is done, there may appear a child of whatever age desired, a one-, three-, seven-year-old and so on, with his emotions and experiences completely unmodified by later life development."[4] The time-machine is operated by the doctor's saying to the patient, "You are now — years old." The patient will then speak like a child of that age and, if he writes something, will write in his childish handwriting.

Time magazine once reported on an article in the British *Journal of Mental Science* by Dr. Denys E. R. Kelsey, "a serious British psychiatrist," who claimed that three of his patients undergoing hypnoanalysis had produced birth memories, and even prenatal memories.[5] One woman, reliving her birth in hypnosis, felt that she was choking, that something was bound tightly around her neck. Dr. Kelsey later learned from the woman's mother that her daughter had been almost strangled by the umbilical cord. With scientific scepticism we may wonder whether the young woman had ever been told of this fact and whether the memory was perhaps constructed out of information given her in her childhood. Needless to say, the possibility of evoking natal and prenatal memories through hypnosis is not yet recognized by most psychologists. And psychologists do not give serious consideration to the fantastic claims of Ron Hubbard, the dianetics man, and of the author of *Bridey Murphy*, of having discovered memories of previous incarnations.

Two quotations sum up the opinion of all but a few psychologists today:

Supposedly forgotten incidents may be recalled in exceptional circumstances: in dreams, in the delirium of fever, in somnambulism, in automatic writing, in crystal gazing, in hypnotic states, and in psychoanalysis. —Asher, Tiffin, and Knight[6]

But is anything once learned ever completely forgotten and lost? Some say no, being strongly impressed by the occasional recovery of memories that were thought to be gone forever. Experiences of early childhood have sometimes been recovered after a long and devious search. Persons in a fever have been known to speak the language of their childhood which in their normal state they could not remember at all. Such facts have been generalized into the extravagant statement that "nothing once known is ever forgotten." . . . There is no evidence for any such extreme view. Probably a great deal is forgotten. —Woodworth and Marquis.[7]

The superiority of recall under hypnotism has been tested in a number of experiments. No superiority has been found for nonsense material, but recall of meaningful material (learned before hypnosis) is better under hypnosis. A. M. Weitzenhoffer found as much as 50 per cent better recall of memorized prose and poetry in hypnotic trance. A further generalization made by Weitzenhoffer is that recall is favored by other similar states, all characterized by relaxation—abstraction, free association, "twilight sleep," and simple relaxation.[8] The fact that simple relaxation may substantially increase recall is important.

Forgetting Due to Brain Injury and Other Physiological Causes. From earliest times men must have noticed that when a person survived an injury to the brain he sometimes suffered a greater or lesser loss of memory. The ancient Egyptians performed brain operations and must have learned something about the functioning of the brain. But whatever was learned before the modern scientific era was lost.

One useful by-product of war has been the opportunity granted to medical men to observe the effects of brain injuries. The many operations on the brain in recent times and experimental operations on the brains of animals have contributed a great deal to our knowledge of the relation between brain injury and memory. It is certainly true that a brain injury does not necessarily result in noticeable amnesia. About 1900, in a Connecticut town, an explosion hurled a crowbar through the frontal region of a workman's brain. At this time it was the general belief that any injury to the brain would be fatal. But the man recovered and lived a long time. No effect of the injury was noticed—unless, as some said, the man had a tendency thereafter to be impatient and bad-tempered.

The brain seems to be able to take a good deal of punishment. Not long ago a young New York housewife shot her husband in the head four times. He lived to beg the court to be merciful to his wife.

Using F. L. Well's memory test, G. L. Beble found that brain surgery produced no permanent, only temporary, amnesia.[9] But Morrow and Cohen, as has already been mentioned, found war veterans with brain injuries to have memory deficiencies.[10] And W. C. Halstead, comparing individuals who had suffered frontal lobe injuries with normal persons, found the former to have poorer memories.[11]

Amnesia (usually partial) may result from various diseases, among them syphilis, epilepsy, and Korsakoff's disease (resulting from alcoholism). Dr. Karl Menninger, in The Human Mind, tells of a middle-aged woman in excellent physical health who had lost practically all her memory, being not quite sure of her own name, through Alzheimer's disease.[12]

The administering of nitrous oxide ("laughing gas"), formerly much used in dentistry and minor operations, has in a few cases damaged memory, the cause being, not the gas itself, but the low oxygen content of the gas mixture.

In 1931 the German psychologist Gustav Störring reported a curious case. After being overcome by gas fumes a man lost all sense of time and the ability to retain the memory of new experiences, his memory span being limited to about two seconds. He married after the accident, but regarded his wife as his fiancée and each time he saw her he treated her as if they had just met after a long separation. He retained some memory of his life before the gas poisoning. We might infer that while deprived of oxygen some of the cells of the brain died.[13]

One experimenter, using himself as a guinea pig, reduced his oxygen supply while attempting to observe the effects of oxygen deprivation. He remembered that he wanted to watch the color of his lips, but he could not remember the difference between the front and the back of the mirror![14]

Nowadays people are sometimes brought back to life after being dead (that is, without heartbeat) for a brief period. But the revived person may take up life again with defective memory and intelligence. If circulation of the blood through the brain is blocked too long, moreover, the mind is totally and permanently destroyed.[15]

Senile Forgetting. We may observe in old people some loss of memory, especially about matters of no great importance. We may note that as Mother grows older she makes more mistakes in spelling and her punctuation becomes rather irregular. Sometimes memories grow a bit confused, as when Grandpa calls his grandson John "Fred" and his grandson Fred "John."

When there is deterioration of memory with age, the cause may be partly physiological and partly psychological. If an old person forgets many things he wants to remember, the cause is probably physiological; if he forgets things because they no longer matter to him, the cause is psychological. Usually both causes operate.

It is well known that old people frequently have an excellent memory for the events of their childhood and youth. This fact is consistent with the evidence that brain damage usually affects memory for recent events more than for earlier events. But there is the additional factor that old people often have little or no interest in the present or future and find their satisfaction in recalling the happier experiences of childhood and youth. If old people lose interest in life, they dismiss most of their memories as of no value. Our humble servant the mind forgets as soon as possible what we do not care to remember.

Since memories tend to grow weaker with the passage of time

unless they are reviewed or used occasionally, we might expect that a great deal of knowledge accumulated in early life would fade away in old age. But an old person usually suffers little loss of memory for a subject in which he is still vitally interested.

People age at various speeds and in various ways, losing one ability while retaining others. Dr. Karl Menninger, in *The Human Mind*, relates a case of early senility. At the age of about fifty-five a prosperous merchant found himself unable to recall the names of important customers. Within a few years he was unable to find his way about the town in which he had spent his life. Dr. Menninger attributed the man's loss of memory to hardening of the arteries of the brain.[16]

On the other hand, centenarians are sometimes physically strong, with keen senses, and mentally alert. E. V. Cowdry, in *Problems of Aging*, describes a man of 106:

He had his memory and other mental faculties particularly perfect to the last, being enabled to discourse about ordinary affairs of his business and common concerns of his life without any hindrance arising from want of recollection or incapacity to form a just opinion on the subject submitted to his consideration.[17]

Edison did some of his best work in his seventies. Goethe completed the second part of his *Faust* when over eighty. Victor Hugo died at eighty-three, writing excellent poetry and carrying on unplatonic love affairs to the very end. Titian painted his masterpiece, the "Pietá," at eighty-five. Shaw retained his extraordinary mental alertness until his death at ninety-four. In May, 1957, Dr. Maurice J. Lewi, founder of the New York College of Podiatry, died at ninety-nine; he had been active in his profession and an excellent speaker until his death. Old people retain their memories and other mental powers when endowed with superior vitality and interest in life.

A number of scientific studies have been made of the relation between age and learning ability, which depends primarily upon memory. Carl I. Hovland sums up the results in the *Handbook of Experimental Psychology* as follows:

From maturity to old age most studies show a continuous decline in speed and accuracy of learning. . . . It is difficult to know how much of the decline is attributable to changes in learning ability and how much to differences in motivation. A widely quoted investigation of learning during adulthood is that of Thorndike et al. [Adult Learning, 1928] They concluded that considerable decline occurs in those of the tests designed to measure "basic modifiability," but that in school subjects the learning of older subjects [people] shows relatively little decline. The absence of decline in the latter [school subjects] is explained as perhaps being due to greater motivation and increased organizing skill.[18]

Unless there is an incapacitating deterioration of mental powers, older people in business or professions compensate for some loss of memory by their superiority in experience, accumulation of knowledge, organizing ability, and mental grasp or broad comprehension.

Active, or Defensive, Forgetting. It is indeed fortunate that we can forget; it is as necessary to forget as it is to remember. I am not speaking now of forgetting unhappy memories, but rather of forgetting what is irrelevant to the purpose of the moment. We could not concentrate on anything at all if we were not able to forget everything else for the time being. The innumerable little insignificant events of daily life and the many facts that come to our attention (as when we look through a newspaper) have to be forgotten, so that our minds can be cleared for action.

Pavlov was one of the first men to find evidence of *active* forgetting. Having discovered that a dog would learn to associate the sound of a bell with food and would salivate upon hearing the bell, Pavlov tried the experiment of withholding food when the bell was rung. Rather quickly the dog unlearned the association and ceased to salivate when hearing the bell. But if, after a certain period of time without any bell-ringing, Pavlov again rang the bell, on this occasion the dog would salivate, showing that the old memory was retained. It is clear that after being disappointed a number of times in his expectation of food after the dinner bell, the dog had put the memory of the bell out of his mind but had not completely forgotten it. Pavlov called this withholding of a memory when the memory is not rewarded *extinction* and attributed it to what he called *internal inhibition.*

Nowadays it is a matter of common popular knowledge that forgetting is often active, but this knowledge is due to Freud rather than Pavlov. When we cannot recall something that we know very well, we often look for a "Freudian" reason.

In 1898 Freud published a short essay called "On the Psychic Mechanism of Forgetting," and in 1901 used the material of the essay, with new material, in his fascinating, famous, and influential book *Psychopathology of Everyday Life*. (In his late work *A General Introduction to Psychoanalysis* the same material is presented in Part I, "The Psychology of Errors.")

Most of Freud's complicated explanations of instances of forgetting are too long for quoting, but the following samples clearly illustrate the underlying assumption that unpleasant things are often barred from consciousness. One instance he quotes from Jung:

"Mr. Y. falls in love with a lady who soon thereafter marries Mr. X. In spite of the fact that Mr. Y. was an old acquaintance of Mr. X., and had business relations with him, he repeatedly forgot the name, and on a number of occasions, when wishing to correspond with X., he was obliged to ask other people for his name."[19]

Another instance, Freud quotes from an account given him by "a young man":

"A few years ago there were misunderstandings between me and my wife; I thought her too cold, and though I willingly acknowledged her excellent qualities we lived together without affection. One day, on coming in from a walk, she brought me a book which she had bought me because she thought it would interest me. I thanked her for her little attention, promised to read the book, put it among my things and never could find it again. Months passed by and occasionally I thought of this derelict book and tried in vain to find it. About six months later my dear mother . . . fell ill. My wife left our house to go and nurse her mother-in-law, who became seriously ill, giving my wife an opportunity of showing her best qualities. One evening I came home full of enthusiasm and gratitude towards my wife. I walked up to my writing desk and opened a certain drawer in it, without a definite intention but with a kind of somnambulistic sureness, and there before me lay the lost book which I had so often looked for."[20]

Freud relates this experience:

I was once the guest of a young married couple and heard the young wife laughingly describe . . . how the day after the return from the honeymoon she had called for her sister and gone shopping with her . . . while her husband went to his business. Suddenly she noticed a man on the other side of the street and, nudging her sister, said, "Look, there goes Mr. K." She had forgotten that this man had been her husband for some weeks. A shudder went over me as I heard the story, but I dared not draw the inference. Several years later the little incident came back to my mind after this marriage had come to a most unhappy end.[21]

Sometimes the forgetting is complicated by a substitute memory, resulting in a "Freudian slip." Here is one of Freud's examples:

A professor of anatomy at the end of his lecture on the nasal cavities asks whether his class has thoroughly understood it and, after a general reply in the affirmative, goes on to say: "I can hardly believe that that is so, since persons who can thoroughly understand the nasal cavities can be counted, even in a city of millions, on one finger . . . I mean, on the fingers of one hand."[22]

A young Communist was acting as chairman of a meeting of a supposedly noncommunist organization. When a matter under discussion was ready for a vote, he said: "We will now vote on the revolution—I mean resolution."

"Freudian" awareness existed before Freud. Charles Darwin, when collecting evidence for his theory of evolution, made it a rule to write down immediately any evidence contrary to his theory, for he knew that otherwise he would probably forget it.

At the beginning of his career as mind doctor, Freud discovered the central role of childhood experiences in the individual's life history. He found that people could, by a great deal of effort and with a great deal of encouragement, recall childhood incidents that had been forgotten but had had a lasting and damaging effect upon their lives. And he also found that these memories had to be brought out of darkness against the resistance of the patient. He soon formulated the theory of repression: that certain memories are thrust out of consciousness because they are too disturbing to be admitted.

The theory that unpleasant things tend to be forgotten (held by Thorndike as well as Freud) has been put to the test. Either the best experimental techniques to examine this topic have not been discovered or the Freudian hypothesis has defects, for the experimental results are equivocal.* The results of many tests show: (1) that as a rule pleasant things are remembered better than unpleasant things but there is not a great quantitative difference; (2) that both pleasant and unpleasant things are remembered better than indifferent things; and (3) that some people ("pessimists") tend to remember unpleasant things and forget pleasant things. Whatever the results of such tests, repression is a fact and recognition of its existence is here to stay.

The most striking instances of loss of memory due to the desire to forget are the cases of sudden and almost total, but usually

---

* Also, most of the subjects of psychologists' tests are presumably normal, whereas all of the psychoanalysts' patients are mentally ill.

temporary, amnesia which are frequently reported in the newspapers. One young man, found sleeping in a bus station in
Detroit, said at the hospital: "It was just like I was born right
there where I stood." (Actually, however, the amnesiac retains
all his memories but the memories of his personal life.)

What happens in such cases is apparently that the person finds
his situation intolerable and the need to escape becomes over-
whelming. Running away would be one solution, but not a wholly
satisfactory one, since the person would carry with him his
memories and the anxieties they create. Forgetting everything is
the most complete escape, except for death.

When the individual has forgotten all his past life he finds
this situation disturbing and so he has a motive for wanting his
memory back. Sometimes it returns quickly. One man who had
wandered, in his amnesia, from New York to California was
identified and returned to his home. He talked to his wife as if
to a stranger, but suddenly called her by the familiar name of
"Peg." At the sound of this name his memories began to return,
through the process of association, and within an hour he had
fully recovered his normal memory.

Limited amnesia is seen in the newspaper account of a man
who wanted to get married but who could not remember whether
or not he had been married before. An inquiry to the probate
judge of his home town brought the information that he had
indeed been married only a few years earlier.

Amnesia on a small scale is often found in connection with
crimes. The person who has committed the crime testifies that
he "blacked out"—that is, has no recollection of doing what he
is accused of doing. Obviously this amnesia is protective.

Sometimes when memories are repressed, they are replaced by
substitute memories which fill the gap. A man is fired from a job
for incompetence or misbehavior; a year later, with another job
he likes, or pretends to like, better, he credits himself with good
judgment in "quitting" the other job. A boy flunks out of college
and not long after, his father has a heart attack; the rest of his
life he bewails his misfortune at having to leave college because
of his father's illness.

"'I did that,' says my memory. 'I could not have done that,'
says my pride, and remains inexorable. Eventually—the memory
yields."—Nietzsche, in *Beyond Good and Evil.*

Everyone has a certain, often rather exalted, conception of himself; things he has done that do not harmonize with this self-image are a thorn in the flesh; so repression steps in and throws the memory down into the dark cellar of the unconscious, or if the memory is too strong to be thrown out it is disguised and dressed up so as to be more presentable. (This is a description of normal behavior, but not everyone behaves in this way; the self-torturer dwells on his mistakes and wrongdoings, even magnifies them.)

George Bach made a study of "redefinitions" in a group of patients being treated for personality and psychosomatic disorders. When these people first appeared for treatment, Bach had them report as many of their experiences as they could recall. After a year or more, the recordings were played back to the patients without any explanation of their source, and the patients were asked to classify each incident as (1) pertinent to their own problem, (2) somewhat similar to their own experiences, or (3) not applicable to their situations. Only 52 per cent of the experiences were recognized and acknowledged as their own, 25 per cent were classed as similar to their own experiences, and 23 per cent were completely disowned as not applicable to them.[23]

To sum up, active, or purposeful, or defensive forgetting is of two kinds: (1) It is essential to focus on one matter at a time and to dismiss other matters. We forget innumerable things to prevent overcrowding of our minds with useless or irrelevant memories. Useless memories we try to forget permanently; irrelevant memories we try to forget temporarily. (2) Normally we tend to forget anxiety-creating memories, or if they can't be forgotten, to alter them so as to make them more acceptable. Extremely harmful results spring from the repression, in childhood, of guilt-creating memories, and mental illness is often cured or alleviated by the recovery and realistic consideration of these memories.

Forgetting through Disuse. The most common notion about forgetting is that it is a "fading," or wasting away. Perhaps even active forgetting may be regarded as due to intentional disuse.

The ability to recall is lost much more quickly than the ability to recognize learned material.

Memories fade away rapidly (as regards recall) when they are not reviewed or used, especially if the individual does not expect

to use them at some later time. E. T. Layton, studying the forgetting of elementary algebra, found that in one year of disuse
pupils lost, on the average, two-thirds of their algebraic knowledge.[24] E. B. Greene, using the subjects of psychology, zoology,
and biochemistry, found that half of the material learned was
forgotten between June and October.[25] But R. I. Watson found
that students he was able to test over a period of five years never
completely lost their knowledge of elementary psychology. Losses
in recognition were slower and more regular than losses in recall.[26]

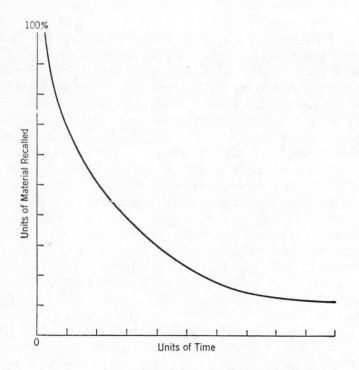

Learning that we cannot recall has probably not entirely disappeared. Numerous experiments with relearning have shown that
a "forgotten" subject can be relearned in less time than was
required for the original learning, even after many years' disuse.
The amount of "savings" in time is a measure of the amount of
retention. And even material that we do not relearn has undoubtedly been transformed into attitudes and values that form the
foundations of our judgment. Education pays in spite of all that
is forgotten.

Forgetting is much more rapid at first. The great German psychologist Hermann Ebbinghaus (1850-1909), who was the first to use nonsense syllables for learning experiments (to avoid the associations of meaningful material), was also the first to construct a *curve of forgetting*. Whatever the kind of material, the curve of forgetting resembles a playground slide, steep at the top and leveling off at the bottom. The diagram on page 38 is merely illustrative, not an actual curve based on an actual experiment. The steepness of the curve at the top is characteristic of the forgetting of nonsense material.

Ebbinghaus was his own subject in his memory experiments. In one typical experiment he learned, one after the other, twelve lists of thirteen nonsense syllables each, considering each list learned when he could repeat it twice without error.[27] He then relearned the lists seven times after various intervals and recorded the time required for each relearning. He considered the percentage of time saved at each relearning when compared with the original learning time as a good indication of the amount of retention. This is what he found:

Time from First Learning to Relearning	Per Cent of Material Remembered (Savings)	Per Cent of Material Forgotten
20 min.	58	42
1 hr.	44	56
9 hrs.	36	64
24 hrs.	34	66
2 days	28	72
6 days	25	75
31 days	21	79

The experiment shows that forgetting starts rapidly and then slows down. Another thing to be considered is that the amount of remembering shown by the "savings" method is not necessarily *usable* remembering. The fact that you could relearn a thing in less time is of no practical advantage at the moment if you cannot recall anything about it.

Nonsense syllables are largely forgotten in a very short time— 42 per cent of 156 syllables in twenty minutes in the experiment described above. The more meaningful the material—that is, meaningful for the learner—the better it is remembered. R. A.

Davis and C. C. Moore compared retention, measured by savings, for 18 studies of meaningless material and 24 studies of meaningful material; after a year they found a little over 60 per cent retention for meaningful material and slightly over 30 per cent for meaningless material.[28]

Madorah Smith tested her recall of material learned in childhood after intervals of twenty-four and sixteen years. Between her eighth and fourteenth birthdays she learned the Westminster Shorter Catechism, consisting of 107 questions and their answers, learning the answer to one question each Sunday—with review, so that at fourteen she knew the whole Catechism perfectly. Twenty-four years later, with no practice in the interim, Miss Smith had herself tested; she recalled 54 of the answers perfectly, needed prompting with one or two words on each of 44 questions, and had to be given considerable prompting on 9 questions. After a lapse of sixteen years, she was retested, and this time she gave 53 of the answers without error, needed prompting with a word or two on 39 questions, and required more prompting on 15 questions. The results of this unique experiment are consistent with the well-established fact that, after a lengthy period of retention, forgetting proceeds very slowly.[29]

Motor learning seems to be retained better than verbal learning. A friend of mine recently bought a bicycle for his son. He mounted the bicycle himself and was able to ride it without difficulty although he had not been on a bicycle for twenty years. R. S. Woodworth tells of a student who after two hundred hours of practice on the piano stopped practicing for a year. At the end of that time he regained his skill in one hour of practice.[30]

E. J. Swift reports having retained 67 per cent of his typing speed after two years without typing practice. He attributes the high degree of retention to the fact that a motor act has to be completely done to be done at all and so requires a higher degree of organization than that required by other kinds of learning.[31] Also favorable to retention is the fact that motor learning is often overlearning.

The well-known statement of Paderewski is sometimes quoted in relation to the need for practice of a motor skill: "If I do not practice for one day, I know it; if I do not practice for two days, my friends know it; and if I do not practice for three days, the audience knows it." This statement, however, deals with peak performance and is a rather special case.

Forgetting through disuse is normal and unavoidable, and there is no reason for you to blame yourself or your memory when it occurs. The mind is a marvelous instrument, but it is not, and cannot be made into, a perfect instrument. Even memory experts, who make a profession of remembering certain kinds of facts in public, forget miscellaneous things just as other people do.

Forgetting Due to Interference. Forgetting was formerly thought to be mainly the result of disuse, but now it is believed that disuse may be a less important factor than interference.

Interference with attention, learning, and remembering may be emotional or intellectual or both. We shall consider emotional interference first.

Emotion can operate either as a guard against interference or as an interference. The story is told of Henry Clay that he wished to make a brief statement in the Senate on a point under discussion. He asked a neighboring Senatorial friend to nudge him after five minutes. The friend nudged in vain and finally drew blood with a pin, but Clay went right on speaking. Afterwards he asked his friend angrily why he had not been stopped. This story illustrates the way emotions may act to prevent interference. Now consider an example of emotion as interference: A young Englishman drove his car to London and to the registry office, to meet his bride and get married. They left London for their honeymoon by train. Two weeks later the young man remembered his car.

A powerful emotion such as love can render the mind virtually incapable of dealing with other matters. "Since I've been with you, can't concentrate," says a popular song. Falling in love has temporarily nullified the value of attending school for many high-school and college students. Emotional disturbances and anxieties are among the most important factors in academic failure, not only for older students, but even for grade-school children. Many children with excellent IQ's cannot learn to read because of such deep-seated anxieties. They cannot concentrate on their studies because they are concentrating on their personal problems.

Other, less romantic, emotions also act as interference. It has been found that emotional drivers constitute one of the major causes of automobile accidents. The angry driver, for example, is apt to be thinking about the quarrel he has had with someone instead of remembering to watch the road and drive carefully.

Stage fright is a common experience. A little boy was asked

by his teacher to learn a poem beginning, "I remember, I remember, The house where I was born," in order to recite it before the class. He was an extremely timid child and had not been long in the school; the thought of reciting a poem in the presence of his classmates terrified him. He had no trouble learning the poem and practiced it repeatedly before the occasion. When he was called on to recite he marched to the front of the room and faced the class. He began, "I remember, I remember"—and that was all he remembered. In stage fright, one has difficulty remembering because of the anxiety created by the situation—the dread of failure (as in an audition or on an opening night), the intense awareness of being the object of the critical attention of strangers. The energies of the mind are occupied in combating fear, so that it is not possible to concentrate wholly on the performance itself.

C. Burri performed an experiment which showed that the presence of strangers caused interference with memory. He tested recall, for previously learned material, of college students with and without an audience of two men and two women. He found that this audience of four strangers hindered recall, and the effect was the same whether the audience showed interest in the proceedings or occupied themselves with other matters.[32]

Ernest Montague studied the effect of anxiety on serial rote learning. He discovered that if the learning problems were difficult, anxiety interfered with learning, but if the tasks were easy, the anxious learners surpassed the more placid ones.[33]

Absent-mindedness is the result of concentration—on something else. The proverbial absent-minded professor who puts out the clock and winds the cat is, of course, deeply preoccupied with a serious problem, and the clock and the cat suffer the results of interference.

The story is told that Albert Einstein once came to New York City to attend a dinner to be given in his honor. He arrived at the hotel early and went out for a walk. After walking for a half-hour, meditating no doubt on weighty problems of advanced physics, he suddenly realized that he was lost. He could not remember the name of the hotel. The police kindly took the matter in hand, telephoning to the principal hotels until they located the one in which the dinner was being held. It appeared that Dr. Einstein had merely walked several times around the block, for the hotel was right in the middle of the block where he had lost his way.

One need not be intellectual to be absent-minded. A New York City housewife who went to the butcher shop to buy meat at closing time found that she had brought home a package of money. Apparently, the butcher had been thinking about closing up and going home and had handed the woman the day's receipts instead of her meat.

The story is told of a man who went upstairs to his bedroom to put on evening clothes for a social occasion. He took off his business clothes, all the time being preoccupied with a problem that had concerned him that day at the office. When completely undressed, he put on his pajamas, went to bed and to sleep. Here defensive forgetting played a part; he was tired and he did not want to attend the social affair.

Emotion and intense concentration on one problem do not exhaust the possibilities of interference. There is purely intellectual interference, the result of mental overcrowding.

Since the invention of printing, civilized man has had to swim in an ever expanding ocean of knowledge. Newspapers, magazines, and books and all the complexities of modern life immerse us in a flood of facts and ideas. To function successfully in business or any profession requires mastery of a great deal of knowledge; furthermore an educated, intelligent person feels a desire and an obligation to know as much as possible about politics, economic and other social problems, the sciences, literature, and other arts. To do this effectively will require all our resources of memory. We must forget the irrelevant, the useless, and the trivial. We must reflect on our reading and our experiences in order to organize and synthesize them. We must so clarify and associate our ideas that they become distinctive and do not interfere with each other. The more we know, the more we are able to learn, provided we keep our mental digestion good by thoroughly examining, understanding, and assimilating everything we take in. Above everything, we must avoid pushing, "cramming," and overcrowding our learning hours with unorganized material.

Forgetting caused by later learning is called *retroactive inhibition*. A good many studies of this factor have been made. Back in 1900 G. E. Müller and A. Pilzecker found that their subjects could remember 56 per cent of material learned after a period of idleness but only 26 per cent if mental activity occurred between learning and testing.[34] John A. McGeoch set 24 college girls to learning nonsense syllables in work periods interrupted by the reading of college humor; he found that the interpolated activity produced "a high degree of retroactive inhibition in terms of both recall and relearning."[35]

There is more interference between two similar subjects than between two unlike subjects; that is, memory for a history lesson would not be much damaged if the study of history were followed by study of chemistry, but there would be considerable interference if study of American history were followed by study of English history.[36]

R. H. Waters and Z. E. Peel found that similarity in methods of learning also resulted in retroactive inhibition.[37]

Since we cannot be awake without thinking, it should follow that there is more loss of memory for learned material when one is awake than when one is sleeping. J. G. Jenkins and K. M. Dallenbach tested this hypothesis. They had two students learn nonsense syllables before sleeping and also before normal daytime activities; they retested the students after intervals of one, two, four, and eight hours. After an hour of sleep the two students could recall 71 per cent and 70 per cent of the syllables learned; after an hour of daytime activities, 44 per cent and 48 per cent. After eight hours of sleep they remembered 55 per cent and 58 per cent; after eight daytime hours, only 4 per cent and 14 per cent.[38] Next to sleep, nonintellectual activities like exercise, music, dancing, or other forms of recreation cause least interference with remembering what has been learned.

There is also proactive inhibition. P. I. Whitely and A. B. Blankenship carried on some experiments in which they found that previous learning interfered with subsequent learning. Interference was greatest for similar subjects, as memorizing one poem followed by memorizing another poem.[39] So there is interference coming and going.

Life, it seems, should be organized, and one should pass through it with a degree of deliberation. There should be rest periods at intervals to allow the brain to lie fallow. Continuous undifferentiated activities apparently fight for a place in the memory, and some things are pushed out and forgotten. A person with a commendable greed for knowledge, who reads book after book as rapidly as possible without organizing the information will lose most of his knowledge to the demon Interference.

A peculiar type of interference is that called blocking. It occurs when one wishes to recall some item which he knows quite well but cannot recall. This situation frequently arises with names. One person reported trying to recall the name of Mr. Rheinweld and being unable to do so because the name Rheingold came to mind and "got in the way."

In cases of this kind, Mr. Rheinweld cannot be remembered until Mr. Rheingold is got rid of. Trying to drive Rheingold out by force does not work; it just makes the name more vivid and stubborn. The thing to do is to say "A plague o' both your houses!" and relax. Mr. Rheingold will sooner or later slip into oblivion and the way will be clear for Mr. Rheinweld to come in. And if you want to prevent future blocking for this name you can link the two names by an association, such as "Gold can be welded, and Rheingold can bring up Rheinweld."

Forgetting Due to Changed Cues. When the right cue is missing, you may have all the information you need stored away in your mind somewhere but be unable to get at it. Students who complain after a test that they knew something but could not think of it are often telling the truth.

Experiments have shown that material is best remembered in the situation in which it was learned.

One who learns material with too great dependence upon the phraseology of the textbook may be at a loss to remember some of the material if he cannot recall the exact wording of the text. For this reason it is better to learn facts and ideas naked rather than in the verbal clothing in which they first came to your attention.

Book learning is not always easily applied to situations outside the classroom. One can learn to identify leaves, flowers, and birds by means of accurate pictures and descriptions, but have difficulty recognizing them on a field trip.

Recognition of people is made difficult by the way in which they change their clothes, their hair, and their expressions. Just a change in location is confusing. You may know Mr. Jones very well in the office but pass him on the street without recognizing him.

Forgetting by Completing. One of the most pleasant ways of forgetting things is to finish them. When they are dismissed as of no further value, memories rush out of the mind like children after school.

A mother of several children was taking graduate courses in education. For one course she wrote a paper on high-school sororities. It was a scorching indictment of these organizations, containing fourteen reasons why they should be abolished. About a year and a half later, her oldest daughter received three bids from high-school sororities. The mother retained her dislike of the sororities, but she could not remember one argument against them from her paper. She had dismissed the whole subject from her mind as a task completed. Too often it happens that we dismiss memories as of no further value and then later—too late—want them back.

CHAPTER V

Memory Improvement —
General Principles

If you have read the two preceding chapters carefully, you should have some understanding of the nature of memory and its opposite, forgetting. This background knowledge should be of value to you as you now study methods of improving memory. In this chapter we shall consider a number of general principles that apply to all learning and remembering. In Chapter VI we shall consider specific techniques of study, practical for both school and adult life. In Chapter VII we shall examine certain memory devices or systems (including those used by professional memory experts). In Chapter VIII we shall give our attention to certain memory problems, such as remembering to do things, remembering faces and names, and memorizing literature and speeches.

Interest. A young man remarked that he had a rather poor memory for things in general, but that for some strange reason his memory for blueprints was excellent. If he took a good look at a blueprint and then saw it again years later, he would know immediately whether it had been altered. A little questioning indicated that his remarkable memory for blueprints was not at all strange. Since boyhood he had been making miniature sailing ships, and it had been necessary to make a blueprint for each one. His exceptional memory for blueprints was a result of intense interest and practice.

You no doubt recall (from Chapter I) other instances of remarkable memories for certain subjects that resulted from a special interest in those subjects. The chances are that if you are intensely interested in something, you have no memory problem in regard to that thing.

On the other hand, it is difficult to learn anything in which you are not interested and more difficult to retain it for long after you have learned it. Nonsense syllables are quickly forgotten because, having no meaning, they fail to awaken interest. People who memorize nonsense syllables are able to do so because they have an indirect or derived interest in them. Ebbinghaus spent years learning them because he was deeply interested in finding out more about the processes of learning and remembering.

Almost any field of knowledge you can think of is nonsense for some people. Children generally lack sufficient understanding of the requirements of adult life to appreciate the value of learning the multiplication table. They perform the task in order to please teachers and parents, to win approval and to escape disapproval or punishment. Many high-school students learn algebra or Latin for the same reason. Some educators have believed that children should not study any subject until they feel a desire to learn it, but the educational system creaks along as best it can, attempting to make the children interested in their subjects, and, when this fails, relying on reward-and-punishment motivation.

What are you to do when you face the task of learning something in which you are not at all interested?

It might be of some help to realize that in order to be interested in a subject you must know something about it and that the more you learn about a subject the more interesting it becomes. If a boy has no postage stamps, he is not interested in stamp collecting. If someone gives him a few foreign stamps, his interest is aroused. If his father then buys him a packet of a thousand different stamps and an album to put them in, the boy may soon become enthusiastic about stamps. If a person knows little or nothing about law, he is not interested in law; but if he reads a popular book on the subject, he will discover that law is a fascinating subject. Think, now, of your best friends and of people you have been in love with—and of your first impressions of them. Is it not true that some of them seemed uninteresting or even unattractive before you got to know them well? Knowledge creates interest, interest leads to more knowledge, more knowledge to more interest, and so on ad infinitum. So why not give an "uninteresting" subject a chance?

The other possibility, when for some reason you are required to study a subject that bores you, is to keep reminding yourself of the advantages of learning it and the disadvantages of not learning it. In other words, strengthen and utilize your indirect, or secondary, interest in the subject. If, using reward-and-punishment motivation, you make a serious attempt to master the subject, you will probably find that you are becoming more interested in it as you learn more about it.

Selection. As you look out over a landscape, you note certain outstanding features—a river, a mountain, a railway, a red roof, a tall factory chimney. If you remember the scene, it will be by recalling these "high spots." In learning any kind of subject matter, it is necessary to concentrate on the high spots, the most significant things. It is impossible to master any subject in all its details.

The great Dutch scholar Erasmus once said that a good memory should be like a fisherman's net—that is, it should retain all the big fishes but let the little ones escape.

We have to use judicious selection daily in many of life's activities. When we eat in a restaurant we order only what we want most and what we can actually eat. When we enter a department store we do not look at everything the store contains; we confine our attention to a few departments where there is or may be something we want to buy. When we "read" a newspaper we do not actually read much of it; we skip whole pages and sections, glance at the headlines, skip the articles that do not interest us, skim or read parts of other articles, and read thoroughly only those items that interest us most. We should use the same kind of judicious selection in learning.

The days of the scholar who took all knowledge for his province are gone. There is so much knowledge in the world today that no one can be well informed in more than a few areas. A person who tries to remember everything becomes bewildered and loses a great deal of his knowledge. But if he restricts himself to a reasonable number of facts, knowledge of these will help him to remember additional related facts.

Specialization has become the order of the day. If a boy is interested in science, he has to decide after a while what science he will pursue; then, after a general grounding in the science, he has to decide what branch of the science to specialize in; and, later, he will have to confine his efforts to one small subdivision of this branch. (For example, science→biology→botany→flowering plants→composite family→goldenrods.)

In the little area you have staked out for your own career, you want to learn, retain, and be able to recall as much as possible. In this area you want the big fishes and the little fishes, too.

By selecting a field of interest for intensive cultivation of knowledge, a person can make his memory do remarkable things for him. You studied at least one language in high school or college. Probably you worked hard at it, found it difficult, and never mastered it. (A year or two of Spanish in school does not enable you to converse easily or understand what is said to you when you visit Mexico.) But Maximilian Berlitz became so intensely interested in languages that he spent his life studying and teaching them. Before he died he had learned fifty languages! You might be able to master many languages if you became sufficiently interested in languages to devote your life to the subject. The grandson of the founder of the Berlitz schools, Charles Berlitz, if born in another family might have become a businessman, a lawyer, a doctor, a scientist, or an artist, with a smattering of two or three languages. But because as a child he acquired an interest in the specialty of the family, he now knows twenty languages and hopes to equal or better his grandfather's record.

But the specialist, like other people, wants, and needs, to know a great deal about things in general—sciences, philosophy, history, literature, arts, politics, etc. In fields outside one's specialty the only realistic aim is to grasp fundamentals, the important facts and concepts.* A botanist does not read a novel as a literary critic or historian would read it. In acquiring general knowledge one must try to catch some big fish, but let the little ones go.

A special technique of selection is to give your attention, when studying a subject or preparing for an examination in it, to those topics you find difficult to understand or remember. The psychologist Carl Seashore as a young man taught in a "little red schoolhouse" and was expected to take part in spelling bees, a

---

* Helpful summaries of important college subjects are available in the College Outline Series, published by Barnes & Noble, Inc.

popular sport of the time. A son of Swedish immigrants, he was handicapped in English spelling. When he considered the enormous number of English words and their unpredictable spelling, the task of learning them all seemed hopeless. But he knew that the words used were taken from McGuffey's speller. He went through the book, crossing out the words he knew how to spell, gave his attention to the difficult or unknown ones, and found it rather easy to master these.

Now any book you study will contain a great deal of material you already know, some material you can easily recall after one reading, and a great deal of explanatory and illustrative material that you need not try to remember once you have understood it. You should use underlining, marginal lines, stars, arrows, question marks, etc., to mark the things you will need to make a special effort to understand and remember. Then you can review the book, giving most of your attention to these things. If you do not own the book, you can jot down brief summaries in a notebook or indicate certain chapters, sections, or pages for special study.

A good rule for selecting things to remember from your miscellaneous reading (newspapers, magazines, books read for pleasure) is to ask yourself, "What shall I possibly want to remember a month from now? a year from now? ten years from now?" You should consider the possibilities, too, and ask, "How much of this can I remember?" In other words, buy only what you can carry.

Attention. To remember a thing we must learn it, and to learn it we must attend to it. This is not always easy if our attention continually runs off somewhere else. We may be able to do several things at once if some of them are habitual, but we can only attend to one thing at a time—and we have to be alert to do that. We can give very little attention to anything when we are drowsy.

The major problem, then, is to be alert and keep our attention on the task before us. This is usually easy for the person of wide experience, extensive background, or exceptional skill. But the amateur must use determination and will.

You have had this experience: As you are reading, an irrelevant idea intrudes and becomes the object of your attention while your eyes go on looking at the words. Suddenly you become aware that you have been going through the motions of reading for perhaps two or three pages without the faintest notion of the thought. Sometimes when a student is unable to answer the teacher's questions about an assignment, he protests, "But I read every word!" The student may be sincere, but he does not understand that reading is more than looking at words. Reading requires thinking, and so does learning. Learning is impossible when the attention is captured and carried off by a pirate idea.

Often when you say you have forgotten something it would be more correct to say you never learned it, because you never gave it your attention in the first place.

Inattention is often due to lack of interest. If you meet a "Mr. Mumblemumble" and he does not interest you and you do not expect to meet him again, you do not bother to ascertain his correct name. If you do meet him again you say, "I'm sorry, but I've forgotten your name." If you misspell frequently, it is because you have never been sufficiently interested in spelling to look at words carefully. If you cannot remember whether Guatemala is in Central America or South America, you are not interested in Spanish America and have probably never looked at a map of the Western Hemisphere with interest and attention.

Or attention can be good but given to the wrong things. One of the most expensive displacements of attention occurs when one dashes in to learn something without making sure he is learning the right thing. He then becomes burdened with a mistaken response that will interfere with his ever obtaining and maintaining the correct memory.

Starting Right. Second-hand learning from dubious sources is sometimes the cause of errors. You have heard the expression "to gild the lily" and may know that it comes from Shakespeare. But Shakespeare actually wrote "to gild refined gold, to paint the lily." You doubtless know the Biblical saying "Pride goeth before a fall." But your memory is based on hearsay; the Bible actually says, "Pride goeth before destruction and a haughty spirit before a fall."

Your memory for facts can also be based on error. You often hear Chicago referred to as "the windy city" and probably assume that Chicago is the windiest city in the country. Actually, New York has a much higher average wind velocity than Chicago. Mark Twain once wrote that the trouble with people is not their ignorance, but their knowing so many things that "ain't so."

"Education consists mainly in what we have unlearned." (Mark Twain's *Notebook*)

Incorrect learning also occurs in learning to do things. The industrial engineer Frank Gilbreth emphasized the importance of using the right methods in the beginning. He pointed out that often when a new worker is learning a job, he is given a few casual instructions and told to go to work. When the inspector or foreman discovers that he has not done the work properly, he is told to do it again, but the inspector does not pay attention to the incorrect methods that were used.

A pleasant gray-haired woman has been working in a business office in New York for over twenty years. Her duties require her to type for half or more of her working day. She types with one finger of each hand, and her typing takes her twice as long as it should. No doubt when she first had to use the typewriter it was only occasionally and she did not consider it worth while to learn to type properly. Now her two-finger typing is an ingrained habit and she lacks the energy to unlearn the habit and learn to type efficiently.

Sometimes people seem to want to start wrong. J. Mathieu, working in Germany, found that people get into error by what we might call (translating freely from the German) impulsiveness and pigheadedness. Mathieu experimented with maps, charts, drawings, and blueprints. He found that most people, in the beginning, are unable to observe complicated visual material accurately and interpret it. They tend to respond quickly rather than take the time to understand. Furthermore, they prefer positive conclusions even though they are false. And having made up their minds, they dislike to change them or to admit their own ignorance or mistakes. Mathieu found that what he called psychocritical training was very helpful. His subjects looked at designs for long periods of time until they felt they knew them perfectly. Then they reported and were shown the errors that still lingered in their observations. The effect of discovering their continued errors was to startle them into using new and better methods of observation.[1]

One of the most helpful aids in developing a good memory is the determination to be cautious in learning new knowledge and habits. Do things *right* at the start. Concentrate on accuracy, not speed, at the beginning. And get a coach, if necessary. Coaches know in advance what mistakes a person is likely to make and can often ward off these mistakes.

A mistake once learned is repeated until it is strongly entrenched and difficult to eliminate. To learn something wrong and unlearn it and then learn it correctly is triple work.

The psychologist Knight Dunlap invented a rather surprising but effective method of getting rid of bad habits: to practice the error. The principle is to make an unconscious habit conscious by practicing it intentionally, while condemning the habit and planning to break it eventually. Suppose that a person becomes aware that he has a habit of fiddling with his clothes when socially uneasy. When alone he should fiddle with his clothes, saying to himself, "I am fiddling with my clothes. I do it because I am nervous, and it shows everyone that I am nervous. It's a stupid thing to do, and I'm going to stop it." Knight Dunlap called this theory of habit extinction "negative practice."[2]

Various investigations have verified Dunlap's theory. W. N. Kellogg and R. E. White, for example, made an experimental test of the hypothesis. They had three groups of people, with twenty-five in each group, learn a maze, tracing it with a pencil. One group was instructed to repeat every error immediately after it was made, and this group achieved the most rapid progress in learning the maze.[3]

The technique has practical value. Dunlap broke himself of the habit of typing *hte* by typing *hte* several hundred times, reminding himself each time that it was wrong. Since he had been making the error unconsciously, he broke the habit by becoming conscious of it.

When one acquires a skill, the elementary actions become a routine matter and no longer require attention, freeing the power of attention for higher things. Thus, unless the notation becomes extremely difficult, a skilled violinist no longer has to give his attention to placing his fingers on the strings in the right place; he gives his attention to purity of tone and nuances of expression.

When boredom or fatigue bring a lowering of attention, it is better for the learner to take a rest than to continue, for progress can take place only during periods of full attention. J. W. Tilton cites a study by D. W. Taylor in which a group practicing one hour a day on the Morse radiotelegraphic code made as much progress as another group that practiced four hours a day.[4]

Understanding. There are two ways to memorize, though they are often used simultaneously. One is to learn by rote (mechanically); the other is to learn by understanding. Some things, such as the combination to a safe, can be learned only by rote. Others, such as a concept or a theory, can be learned only by understanding. Still other things, such as a poem, can be learned by rote but are learned better by a combination of rote and understanding.

An illustration of the two methods applied to the same task is found in teaching two people of different temperaments and abilities to drive an automobile. One person may have no mechanical aptitude or interest; he may merely want to know what to do to start the car, control it, and stop it. Another person, with mechanical knowledge or aptitude, would want to understand the workings of the hidden parts of the car and what happens when he performs a certain action. The latter person has much more to learn, but he has a more useful skill when he is through. He will understand better how to handle his car in all kinds of novel circumstances, whether it be snow, sand, overheating in the mountains, or driving under the difficult "stop and go" conditions of summer holiday traffic. He will be a more reliable driver in all the unpredictable hazards of the road.

Rote learning of a task can sometimes be taught more quickly, and those who have learned by rote may work faster than those who work by understanding. Therefore rote learning is sometimes better for those who perform rather simple tasks that do not vary much. It is particularly useful when it permits tasks to be done by those with a minimum of training. Understanding proves its superiority when tasks are complicated and varied and when the situation is changed in some way (as by use of a new machine). Of course, the rote learner is helpless if the machine develops quirks or breaks down.

Meaningful learning is retained much longer than rote learning. No one can remember a list of nonsense syllables (for which rote learning is the only possible method) for long without frequent repetition. But meaningful material may be recalled after a lapse of many years. One man who had delivered the senior oration when he graduated from college began to recite it fifty years later and found that he could repeat almost all of it. The psychologist E. B. Titchener learned Milton's poem "On the Morning of

Christ's Nativity" (244 lines) when he was eight years old; at sixty he could recite the poem with very little prompting.

D. D. Droba tested the effect of information on the memory of students for paintings. He divided the students into six groups and gave each group different amounts of information about the pictures. He found that a painting was remembered better when information was supplied about the painter and the painting; the information gave the painting more meaning.[5]

The more associations a thing has, the more meaning it has. Another view is that meaning is synonymous with discrimination and that a person who can make clear distinctions, as an artist does in the field of painting or as a physician does in the field of medicine, will have a good memory for that field. The difference between the ability of an expert to remember the material in his field and the capacity of a novice to remember it is to be explained by the fact that the expert is able to make a great many associations with new data and to relate these data to others by noting similarities and differences.

When it comes to ideas, the thing to do is not merely to memorize a statement from a book but to understand the idea clearly, associate it with other ideas, and put it in its proper place in a larger system of ideas. Once you have done this, remembering the idea requires little effort.

Millions of school children pledge allegiance to the flag. In order for the pledge to mean anything, all the words must be understood—"allegiance," "indivisible," and "justice." Doubtless many children say "one nation invisible, with liberty and just as for all." A New York child was reported as praying "lead us not into Penn Station." We laugh at children's misunderstandings, but college teachers who ask their students the meanings of certain words in their assignments find that they rarely bother to look up in the dictionary words they do not understand. Unless you understand all the words which affect the meaning of a sentence, you do not understand the sentence. And if you do not understand the sentence, you do not fully understand the paragraph.

Says Hans Reichenbach, in his Rise of Scientific Philosophy: "According to Einstein the universe is not infinite, but a closed Riemannian space of a spherical type." Obviously the sentence is entirely meaningless unless you know what a Riemannian space is.

The difficulty of understanding some of the things we read is partly, but not wholly, a matter of unfamiliar words. A little child could easily learn to repeat the statement "Wisdom increaseth sorrow," but he could not have even a glimmer of its meaning. To understand the pledge to the flag fully would require an understanding of such abstract concepts as allegiance or loyalty, a symbol (the flag), a nation, liberty, justice—matters on which many books have been written.

You can hardly derive meaning from learning the names of the geologic eras azoic, archeozoic, etc., unless you know or learn that -zoic means "pertaining to life," a- is a negative prefix meaning "no" or "not," archeo- means "primitive" or "ancient," etc.

Then there is the matter of grammar and sentence structure. A teacher of English literature at New York University found that not one student in a sophomore class could understand Gray's "Elegy Written in a Country Churchyard," which is simple compared to much recent poetry. The difficulty was not mainly a matter of understanding words; it was largely the unfamiliar word order of such lines as:

> Full many a gem of purest ray serene
> The dark, unfathomed caves of ocean bear.

The students did not realize that serene is an adjective describing ray; they could not pick out the subject and the object of the word bear, and it was apparent that some of them were not clear about the difference between a subject and an object.

In the learning of facts and ideas, a bare literal understanding is often of little value. A student can learn that World War I began in 1914. But there is little significance in that fact unless the student has some idea of what the world was like in 1914 and how and why the war happened.

The trouble with much of our learning is that it is not preceded by sufficient background learning. Often an ignorant young person tries to understand something that was written for intelligent, even learned, adults, and naturally fails. Any one of us can run into this kind of difficulty if we try to read something for which we have insufficient background. You can follow the upward path of learning only by taking one step at a time; you cannot fly to an upper level.

In starting a course or a book, it is especially important to understand everything at the beginning, because everything that follows requires understanding of what has come before.

I could not emphasize sufficiently that learning a thing means understanding it. Never be satisfied with learning the form and not the content. Never be satisfied with a hazy idea of what you are reading. If you are not able to follow the thought, go back to where you lost the trail. You cannot remember what you have never known.

Intention to Remember. The bending of one's energies toward a given end is called, by psychologists, *mental set,* and it affects memory as well as other activities. The things we intend to remember are much more apt to be recalled later than other things we observe, hear, or read.

You have seen a great many dollar bills in your life, and you look at every one you pay out to make sure that it is not a "larger" bill. But what do you remember about a dollar bill right now? Whose portrait is on it—Franklin's? Washington's? Hamilton's? or Lincoln's? What are the three colors used? How many signatures are on it? How many complete sentences? What picture is on the back? How many times does the value appear as "1"? as "ONE"? You are doing well if you can answer one of these questions correctly and confidently. You have probably forgotten these things because you do not need to remember them and therefore have never had any intention to remember them. But if you take a notion to ask your friends these questions (in order to feel superior and make them feel inferior), you can easily remember these facts.

Why is it so difficult to establish, by the testimony of witnesses, what actually happened at the scene of an accident or crime? Besides the fact that people, especially when excited, are not skilled observers, there is the important fact that when such a thing happens, witnesses are not thinking about being interrogated later and so are not intending to remember. Otto Leible reported an experiment in a policeman's school. While a class of police cadets were listening to a lecture, two men burst into the room. One made a homicidal attack upon the other. The whole scene, planned and rehearsed beforehand, took six seconds. Immediately the observers were requested to write a description of the affair to which they would be willing to swear. Not one account was free from error. The cadets who watched the scene did not expect to be tested and did not intend to remember what happened.[6]

In a little California town an Armenian immigrant started a pushcart business and in time he owned a store. The man died, and his wife carried on the business; but since she could not write, she kept no books. She was willing to sell on credit and relied on her memory to know who owed her and how much. I spent a summer in this town and at the beginning of the summer bought some items on credit. In order to test her memory I did not offer to pay for them until the end of the summer. The woman knew just what I had bought and what I owed her. Since she had to remember, she intended to remember, and she did.

Evidence of the importance of intention is found in tests of the blind. S. P. Hayes, in a study of 615 teen-age blind children, discovered that they had better memories for material presented orally than seeing children of the same age. His conclusion was that they had better oral memory because they had a greater need to develop it and made a greater effort to do so.[7]

H. H. Remmers found that an intention to retain learned material for three days, one week, and two weeks facilitated recall at the time intended.[8]

The section on "Forgetting by Completing" (Chapter IV, page 45) has some bearing, in a negative way, upon the present topic.

Confidence. When we intend to remember, without having confidence that we can remember, the intention is weakened into mere hoping.

A runner who does not think he can win might as well drop out of the race, for he is beaten before he starts. A child who becomes convinced that he is stupid and cannot learn may really become stupid and be unable to learn. People who think they have poor memories do have poor memories (as regards actual functioning), because they lack the confidence necessary to make the effort to remember. As Thomas De Quincey said, "The memory strengthens as you lay burdens upon it, and becomes trustworthy as you trust it."

We might look at the problem as one of investment. If you are a prudent person, you do not feel like investing your good money in something speculative. The principle applies equally to the investing of time and effort. Faced by a learning task, a person who does not expect to profit from an investment of time and effort does not feel like investing.

Perhaps this is a good place to consider the practice of writing things down or using other devices that relieve the memory of some of its burdens. The principle here is that of avoiding interference, of not breaking up concentrated thinking with distractions. A great many items that attach themselves to a busy life are better "remembered on paper."

If you do not feel confident that you will remember a professor's lecture a month or two later, by all means take notes on it. If you do not feel confident that you will remember the contents of an article that interests you, at some time in the future when you want to remember it, file it. If it would take you longer to memorize a shopping list than to write it down, then write it down (there is nothing to lose, for you would probably have to write it down anyway in order to memorize it). If you must call Mr. Johnson at a specific time and are afraid that you might be engrossed in work at the time or that something might happen to distract you, then, unless you have a secretary who can be relied on to remind you, set the alarm clock for that hour and relax—otherwise, you will not be able to concentrate on other things. (If you are squeamish about coddling your memory, use your written notes as a prompting device. Form the habit of trying to rely on your memory before referring to your written reminders.)

With such practical reservations, however, it remains true that you cannot learn and remember something without the confidence that you can learn and remember it. And the memory should be trusted—within the limits of its trustworthiness. The proper attitude is not "I want to remember" or "I hope to remember" or "I intend to remember," but "I intend to and can remember."

Ego Involvement. The subject of most interest to every human being is himself. One long remembers what has been a part of himself.

President Eisenhower once demonstrated this fact. He was waiting with some friends to throw the switch that would light up an international trade fair in Seattle. The conversation turned to the Morse code, which he had learned forty years before at West Point. He stepped over to the key and tapped out something he remembered well: his own name.

A person's world is a mental construct built around himself, the creator and ruler of that world. All his memories, all his knowledge, and all his ideas are associated with the self. The Second World War is for him not so much an event of history as a complex of his experiences. A certain school of thought is his philosophy.

F. C. Bartlett tells of an African chieftain who visited England. When he went home, his most vivid memory of England was of the traffic policeman with upraised hand—because in his native Swaziland the uplifted hand was a sign of welcome.

Carl J. Warden discovered that students would learn letters, digits, and geometrical designs better if they watched them being written down or drawn, because in this way they acquired a feeling of taking part, of being involved.[9]

A famous comedian once told that he had seventeen trunkfuls of scrapbooks and clippings relating to his career. A German named Hennig, at sixty-three years of age, could recall five thousand dated memories of his life.[10] Everyone keeps "trunkfuls" of memories in his "attic." People who keep and use trunkfuls of facts and ideas are able to do so because they have made these things part of their lives.

It is said that a man complained to Samuel Johnson that he could not remember what he read. "Pray sir," said Dr. Johnson, "do you ever forget what money you are worth, or who gave you the last kick in the shins?" Dr. Johnson was, in effect, telling the man that if he cared as much about what he read as he did about his personal affairs he would remember it.

To some things we are indifferent, but much of what we know could be placed in two categories: things that please us and things that displease us, and (except for defensive forgetting) these things we are likely to remember. The more intelligent and sensitive you become, the more facts and ideas strike you pleasurably or painfully. You become a partisan, not an uncomprehending spectator. Taking sides—in history, in today's political and social problems, in past and present controversies in religion, philosophy, and science—is good for the memory. Ego involvement promotes interest, attention, and intention to remember.

Involving the ego, however necessary it may be, is not without its dangers. Partisanship may be based on insufficient knowledge, and in any case interferes with judgment; cool, rather than hot, thinking is socially desirable.

Gardner Murphy, in a study of personality, describes a learning experiment with American students, in which the material to be learned was in part very favorable and in part very unfavorable to the Soviet Union.[11] The students learned best the material that reinforced their previous opinions.

So we conclude that for maximum learning and remembering, you should involve the ego, but, as the Greeks advised, "nothing too much."

Meaningful Associations. May I remind you that William James pointed out that the more associations made with a fact, the better it is retained in the memory. "Each of its associates becomes a hook to which it hangs, a means to fish it up by when sunk beneath the surface." The man with the best memory, according to James, is the one who thinks over his experiences and who systematically relates and connects his thoughts.

Here are a few examples of the simplest kind of association, in which datum A is associated with datum B:

(1) You can remember where Tasmania is only by associating it with Australia; you can remember Sicily's location by picturing it as being kicked by the boot of Italy.

(2) You associate the units volt, ampere, ohm, with the physicists Volta, Ampère, Ohm.

(3) If you want to remember that Pavlov was the author of the psychological theory of conditioning, always picture Pavlov with a dog, and if you have understood the subject well in the first place, you will be sure to remember his experiments with dogs and his findings and conclusions.

(4) Cervantes died in 1616. Since an English-speaking person who is interested in literature is very likely to remember that Shakespeare also died in that year, he can, through this association, remember when Cervantes died, that Shakespeare and Cervantes were contemporaries, and that the Spanish *siglo de oro* and the Elizabethan golden age were of the same historical period.

(5) A chance association: If you were given the hotel room 1429, you might associate that number with the well-known date 1492, remembering to reverse the last two digits of the date.

When you connect two things in your mind, you do so because they have something in common, but where there are similarities there are also differences, and the differences are as important as the similarities. To associate like things creates confusion unless differences are noted. To associate the words *religious* and *sacrilegious* is hazardous to the spelling of the latter (an additional association with *sacrilege* is needed). Here are a few other examples of associated pairs, in which the differences are very important: Henry James and William James; Louis XIV and Louis XVI; Uruguay and Paraguay; white-crowned sparrow and white-throated sparrow; uranium 235 and uranium 238. If the differences are well understood and learned, the associations are useful.

Linking two things together is a rather elementary form of association. As a rule a thing has many associations. Consider the sunflower. Aside from its botanical significance as a member of the composite family, it may remind you of the "Sunflower State," Kansas. It may remind you of the painter Van Gogh, for whom it was apparently a symbol of the sun, of light, heat, power, life. You may be reminded of the long history of sun worship and solar deities. It may bring to mind the song "Believe Me, If All Those Endearing Young Charms," in which the sunflower is a symbol of devotion. The flower may remind you that its seeds are eaten as food. You may think of the seeds as a source of oil. You may think of bees and of the interrelationships of all living things. You may be reminded of your childhood if you grew up in a region where the great flower is conspicuous—or of seeing the seeds for sale in a Mexican market. All these things add to the significance of the sunflower and assure it a permanent place in your memory.

(The forming of illogical or fantastic associations as a memory device will be considered later.)

Building Background. It is necessary to have a background of knowledge—the more the better—in order to form associations and discern relationships. You cannot understand anything that stands alone; an isolated thing has no meaning. (To paraphrase Donne: no thing is an island.) A seashell would be an incomprehensible, meaningless object to one who had never seen or read about the sea.

Perhaps at some time you have experienced an American Indian dance, a Chinese play, a bullfight, a Balinese orchestral performance, or some other exotic work of art completely foreign to your experience. Or you may have watched a game of cricket or soccer. If so, you realize how little it meant to you—because you had no background of knowledge and experience.

William James explains how a boy who is a baseball fanatic builds background. The boy's interest in baseball impels him to talk about baseball games, to see them when he can, and to think about baseball at frequent intervals. Each thought is a repetition, or review, of its first occurrence, and each review comes in a new setting, bringing new associations. Each time the boy learns of or sees a game, it reminds him of other games. Finally, every player, with his batting average, special abilities, and personal peculiarities, and every team, with its season's score, are tied in with other associations. The whole forms a wealth of systematized knowledge, so that the boy is able to answer any question about baseball instantly.

The baseball fan may retain this baseball memory for life. Not long ago I talked to a college professor who was able to name all the players on the Yankee and Giant teams in the World Series game at the Polo Grounds in 1921. He was thirteen years old at the time, and he "watched" the game on the Brooklyn *Eagle* scoreboard.

It is astonishing to one who has never been interested in baseball that a man could remember such facts for so long a time. A person who has little or no knowledge of a subject is always amazed at the specialist's knowledge of his field. When physicians talk medicine together, they express such extensive and precise observations in such complicated technical language that a layman is flabbergasted. But that kind of memory is possessed by anyone who has specialized in something or other over a number of years.

Because it is a popular superstition that the mind has a limited capacity, like that of a bucket for water, it cannot be repeated too often that the more you know the more you can learn. A well-stocked mind allows more possibilities of association between new material and previously known material. The best way to improve your memory for the data of a subject is to learn more of the data of that subject—in the terms of this section, *build background*.

Organization. A place for everything and everything in its place is the principle that should govern the memory. A good memory is like a well-organized and well-maintained filing system. When a new fact presents itself, the first problem is whether to keep it or throw it away. If the decision is to keep it, the next problem is where to put it. (Deciding where to put it requires, of course, that it be thoroughly understood.) The fact should then be associated with other similar facts already filed. It must be put into a group, or class, of facts and into a certain place determined by its relation to the other facts in the group—that is, its similarities to and differences from related facts. Orderly material put away in an orderly mind seldom gets lost.

Organization is an innate tendency of the mind. A newborn baby soon starts to organize its experiences. It begins to make associations between similar things and things that happen together, and to note differences between similar things. By the time he is a year old the child is distinguishing between himself and other things, between people and things, between people and animals, between live animals and toy animals, between mother and father, between known people and strangers, between things to eat and things to drink, between foods and toys. That is, he is associating experiences into classes, noting similarities and differences between classes of things and between things of the same class. An adult could write a large book containing only what the yearling knows, organizing it logically—and this organization would correspond to the child's own organization, although he has never become conscious that he is organizing and is incapable of comprehending the concept of organization.

As the years pass, the child acquires a large amount of knowledge of his little world, and then goes to school, learns to read, and amasses much knowledge that goes beyond personal experience All of it that he understands he organizes.

By the time the child is in high school, he has learned, even if he is not a good student, a great deal about the world. In his filing system he has a place for the spelling of beautiful, $8 \times 9 = 72$, robins, chocolate ice cream, Abraham Lincoln, jet planes, bathing suits, Egypt, carburetors, 1776, television commercials, thunderstorms, the Empire State Building, kisses, kangaroos, quotation marks, angels, aspirin tablets, lies, footballs, elections, and so on ad infinitum. As he picks up this knowledge he organizes it in simple ways, and the better his understanding the more complete this organization is apt to be.

As long as a person lives he continues to organize his knowledge. He knows a hawk from a handsaw—and he knows a hawk from a pigeon or a seagull, may even know a red-tailed hawk from a sparrow hawk. He may have erroneous and harmful ideas. For example, he may regard a hawk as an enemy of man, as something to be killed. But the source of this wrong classification is wrong information, given him by parents or others who have wrong information. Elementary organization of his world is one of the requirements of being a sane person.

Organization becomes a special problem when the student studies a complicated subject, such as grammar, English history, chemistry, or philosophy. In this situation someone else—a teacher or a writer—must point out similarities and differences and present him with already worked-out classifications.

If we take an abstract, logical point of view, we can look at the learning of a set of related facts as consisting of three processes: (1) learning a large number of facts; (2) making associations between facts on the basis of similarities and differences; (3) organizing the facts into natural and logical groups and relating the groups to each other as parts of larger groupings. But these are not actual chronological stages of learning: from the beginning, all these things are done simultaneously.

Practical memory problems involving classification are:

1. Learning the over-all organization of a subject, that is, learning the major divisions of the subject.
2. Learning a single classification system.
3. Classifying miscellaneous data.
4. Classifying a single item.

If you are a student, studying a course with a textbook, 1 and 2 are your main problems. Try reorganizing some of the simpler concepts and compare your order of items with that given by the author of the textbook. Any increase in your ability to organize information will improve your memory for such information.

The organization of a subject as presented in a textbook is based on logical and pedagogical necessity. Look at the index of the textbook and you will be intrigued with the large number of separate concepts that are presented. If all these concepts were left unconnected, as they are in the index, you would have to work hard in order to understand and remember only a few of them. But in the book, they are carefully organized. Simple facts are subordinated to principles. Like things are compared, unlike things contrasted. Ideas presented first often make it possible to understand subsequent discussions. Parts of a topic are placed in the proper order so that the whole topic becomes meaningful. In short, the textbook is comprehensible and rememberable. Good organization is one earmark of a good book.

One kind of organization which is necessary in some studies is that in which each of a number of groups is contained in a larger group—as in geography and biology. In biology, when we consider an individual organism from the viewpoint of classification, we can place it, schematically, within a series of concentric circles, as illustrated below. The individual at the center is a dog, Mr. Barker.

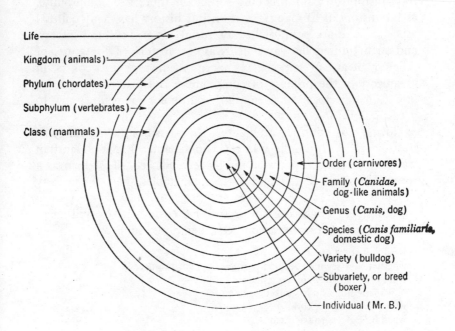

The classification just illustrated is an example of *natural classification*. A classification which is not natural, but which is made for convenience, is an *artificial classification*. An example of artificial classification is alphabetical order, used for dictionaries, encyclopedias, bibliographies, and the like. If you wanted to classify the states of the U.S.A., you might use natural classification, grouping them by regions, as the New England states, etc., or you might use artificial classification, arranging them alphabetically, or by size, population, wealth, etc.

One complicating feature of classifications is that sometimes the dividing lines are not sharp. For example, just when do the "Middle Ages" begin and when do they end? Where is the dividing line between learning and remembering?

Another complication is that classifications may cut across each other. The large subject of history may be divided chronologically, but it is not feasible to study one chronological unit—say, the sixteenth century—with attention to the important events of all the countries and regions of the world. History is usually divided geographically—as Chinese history, Spanish American history, history of California, and so on. Or there is a compromise, as the history of Europe since 1815. But history has many cultural aspects; there are political history, social history, cultural history, and such limited but large fields as the history of literature, of religion, of art, of science. Therefore any history textbook is, in organization, the product of compromise; the historian turns his attention now to an area, now to a chronological period, now to a cultural field.

Now let us consider problem 3, the classification of miscellaneous data. An example was given in Chapter I. Mrs. Hausfrau wants to buy seven items at the grocery. She classifies them as a meat, a frozen vegetable, two raw vegetables, and three dairy products.

A salesman might classify prospective customers, in writing or mentally, according to various considerations, such as:

by alphabetical order
whether they seem to be good prospects or poor prospects
what products they are interested in
how many times he has talked to them
where they live, or work
when he expects to see them
whether they require this or that selling technique
their nationality
whether they are men or women
whether he knows them well or needs to study them
whether he likes them, dislikes them, or is indifferent

Our salesman meets problem 4 when he acquires a new prospective customer. His problem is how to classify him in various ways. He has the problem of thoroughly learning the new human fact—appearance, name, occupation, interests, and so on; of making associations (noting similarities and differences) between the new prospect and others he already has filed away in writing and memory; and of tying all these associations together.

Whatever your memory problem, it becomes easier when you systematically arrange and group your data.

*Whole and Parts.** Since it is not possible to swallow a great deal of knowledge all at once, it is necessary to attack a large subject by nibbling away at it part by part. Still, something is to be said for taking a good look at the whole subject even if you cannot swallow it.

It has been experimentally demonstrated that a poem or piece of prose, if not extremely long, can be memorized more quickly by reading and rereading the whole thing than by working on one small part at a time. The memorizing of literature and speeches will be considered, as a special memory problem, in Chapter VIII. But here it is important to note that the principle involved is applicable to study in general.

If the efficient way to remember a fact is to file it in its proper place, it is of course necessary that there be a place—a subdivision of the filing system in which the fact belongs. This means that one must have the idea of a class of things before he can understand the particular thing and know what to do with it. Thus, in order to make any sense of a swordfish, one would have to have a good idea of the class of fishes.

The concept of the whole plays a dominant and essential role in the learning of any body of knowledge. A body of knowledge might be compared to a huge jigsaw puzzle composed of innumerable small pieces: you cannot assemble them properly without an awareness of the whole picture. The principle is most obvious when applied to organisms and machines, but it applies to even the most abstract subjects.

In order to know the whole you must know the parts, and in order to know the parts you must know the whole.

Dividing and Grouping. In an issue of *Science News Letter,* Dr. George Miller, of Harvard, restated the old belief that college students can remember only about seven separate items from one presentation.[12] Dr. Miller pointed out the significance, as regards memory, of the fact that the number seven appears frequently in man's efforts to organize data, as in the seven days of the

---

* See page 22, "The Importance of Pattern (Gestalt)."

week, the seven wonders of the world, the seven seas. He pointed out the necessity for breaking through the "memory barrier" by the device of classification, or organization. Items are taught and learned in rememberable bunches, and these little bunches of knowledge are tied together with other little bunches into larger bunches.

In other words, knowledge must be ingested like food—in quantities that can be taken in one bite, chewed, swallowed, and digested. Sometimes knowledge comes in large chunks, like a steak, and has to be cut up into bites. Again, knowledge may be presented in very small units, which can best be taken in groups, like peas on a fork.

For example, a number presented as 314829065 is more easily learned and remembered if it is divided into three groups: 314,829,065. And a series of digits 7,2,1,8,6,3,4,9 can more easily be learned if grouped: 7218—6349.

If you meet for the first time the word *anthropomorphic*, you can pronounce it only if you divide it into syllables and you can learn its meaning only by dividing it into its component parts— *anthropo-morph-ic*—and learning the meanings of these parts. (If you are weak on Greek stems, you have to consult the dictionary before you can divide it into meaningful parts.) On the other hand, if the word were spelled out to you—a,n,t,h,r,o,p,o,m,o,r, p,h,i,c—you would have to group the letters into syllables to pronounce the word, and then you would have to group the syllables into meaningful units.

When you learn from a textbook, your intellectual meat is presented cut up for you into bite-size pieces, each of which is a small subdivision of the subject. The instructor uses his judgment as to how many bites you should be able to consume at one meal.

If you wish to learn a number of facts outside of a textbook, you have to use your own judgment as to whether dividing or grouping is called for and as to the size of the divisions or groups. If it is a matter of dividing, you should try to divide the subject according to its natural divisions if it has them, or impose an artificial classification upon it, such as alphabetizing or numbering or some other convenient principle.

Sometimes the processes of dividing and grouping amount to the same thing, the difference being in how you look at your facts. For example, if you wish to learn the names of the fifty states, you may consider them as constituting a unit of knowledge, in which case you divide it; but if you consider them as so many separate facts, you group them. In either case, you probably learn them by six's or eight's.

Here are several examples of typical learning problems in which dividing is an advantage:

The chore of learning the titles of Shakespeare's thirty-seven plays is not so formidable if you learn them in three groups: comedies, histories, and tragedies.

If you want to learn, for ready reference, the names of the Spanish-American countries, this will be fairly easy if you learn them in groups: Mexico and the Central American countries, the Caribbean countries, and the South American countries (dividing the last, largest group into two alphabetical or geographical subgroups).

In order to study biology, it is necessary to learn the following classification system, with the terms in the order given: Kingdom, Phylum, Class, Order, Family, Genus, Species, Variety. Learning these terms is much easier if they are divided into two groups:

Kingdom	Family
Phylum	Genus
Class	Species
Order	Variety

As one increases his mastery of a subject, he develops the ability to combine separate data into ever larger groups. A beginning pianist has difficulty in picking out a melody with his right hand, one finger at a time. When he develops a certain amount of skill, he can strike chords with both hands simultaneously and follow with his fingers an intricate and rapidly changing pattern of notes. A child just starting to read can, after a period of effort and practice, learn to distinguish between cat and rat Years later he will recognize words like categorical and rationalization in a fifth, or less, of a second. And if he becomes an efficient reader, he will be able to read a phrase like categorical imperative at a glance. This ability to handle larger groups of data is, of course, based on understanding and skill developed by practice.

Reinforcement by Repetition and Use. A thing once experienced may be so vivid a memory that it cannot be forgotten even if never voluntarily brought to mind. A fact once learned may be so interesting, so important, so satisfying, or so shocking that no effort is required to remember it—it seems to remember itself. But the ordinary run of little facts, without special significance, cannot long be recalled without attention and effort.

To remember your little fact, utilizing the general principles discussed in this chapter:

(1) try to see its significance, try to be interested in it, or at least in the value of remembering it;

(2) give it your attention, be sure you have it right;

(3) be sure you fully understand it;

(4) intend to remember it;

(5) be confident that you can remember it;

(6) involve the ego, if possible;

(7) associate it with other related facts;

(8) file it in its proper place in your memory system;

(9) see it as part of a larger whole;

(10) if there is a basis for doing so, learn it as part of a small group of related facts.

Then reinforce it by repetition.

Suppose that your little fact is that the German word for *room* is *Zimmer*. You have a much better chance of remembering it if, instead of just looking at it and going on to the next word, you repeat room—Zimmer, or Zimmer—room, ten times (thinking of a room while repeating the word). *Zimmer* will be still more strongly reinforced if after learning all the words in the list in this way you come back to it and see whether it looks familiar and has meaning. But you are not through learning it. You will have some German sentences to translate into English, and in these you will come across *Zimmer* at least once. If you do not immediately know the meaning of the word, more practice by repetition is needed. Then there will be English sentences to put into German, and if the author is not remiss the word *room* will occur several times. By this time you should begin to think of a room as also a *Zimmer*. The word will be further reinforced by occasional use in classroom conversation and in later translation exercises. As long as you speak or read German you will occasionally reinforce your memory of *Zimmer* as *room*. If after your German course is completed you never go to Germany, speak German, or read German, your knowledge of the language will fade, but some words will stay with you, probably the ones you used most.

Things learned, if not of special significance, are ordinarily forgotten after a time if not practiced or used. Whole subjects, like algebra, are forgotten in this way. They may be remembered to the extent that they could be relearned with less time and effort, but they have sunk too far beneath the surface for recall.

CHAPTER VI

Study Methods

This chapter is not only for college students. Many adults who have left their school days behind go right on studying, because they have to or want to. Adults have to learn and remember a great many things even if there are no more examinations. (And there are always the tests of adult life to pass or flunk.) The study methods considered here apply equally to students in school and students out of school.

Adults generally continue to use the study methods they used in college or high school, which is all very well if those methods were good. As a rule students have to develop their own methods based on trial and error and perhaps some good advice from teachers who realize the importance of study methods. The schools require students to do a great deal of studying, but too often they neglect to teach students how to study. When a student fails, his failure is usually attributed to lack of effort or ability. But sometimes study methods make the difference between failure and success. And even for the most capable students good study methods mean better learning with less effort.

Everything discussed in this chapter has to do with learning through reading, and we shall consider only reading for information, not the reading of literature for pleasure.

Of course, interest, attention, and the other matters discussed in Chapter V are of basic importance, but in this chapter such prerequisites for learning will be taken for granted and we shall give our attention to more specific techniques.

The Environment for Study. In order to concentrate on a book it is necessary to eliminate interference so far as possible. You cannot study successfully in a room with a television set in operation. If there is a program you must see, do not try to read at the same time. If other people are viewing and listening to a program that does not interest you at all, you still cannot eliminate the sound or resist taking a look now and then. Some people can concentrate on a book while listening to soft radio music, but the only kind of radio program that does not seriously interfere with study is a long program of instrumental music without interruptions from commentators or commercials.

It is impossible to concentrate completely on a book in a room where a child is playing or adults are talking. The only satisfactory environment for study is a room where you are alone or with another person who is reading—or a library.

If you study in a comfortable chair, especially after a heavy meal or when you have not been getting enough sleep, you may have interference from within—drowsiness. You are wasting your time if you continue looking at pages without being mentally alert. You can either give up and doze or wake yourself up with a little exercise or perhaps a cup of coffee. You can skimp on sleep for a limited time, but sooner or later you have to face the facts of life as regards the necessity for a certain amount of sleep and the inelasticity of the 24-hour day.

It is assumed that you read in a good light, so placed that there is no glare on your page. It is also assumed that your vision is good or is corrected by lenses.

Use of All the Senses. With regard to the senses, we speak of various kinds of memory: visual, auditory, tactual, olfactory, gustatory, muscular, or motor. In remembering experiences we recall sense impressions of several kinds. If you have read Proust's "Overture" to his *Remembrance of Things Past*, you no doubt recall how the taste of the "madeleine" revived a childhood memory for him.

In various kinds of learning it is necessary to use other senses than sight or hearing. In learning physical skills, such as operating a machine, dancing, tennis, or playing the piano, motor and kinesthetic memories play a central role.

The device of verbalizing motor learning has been found useful.

Infantrymen and marines are advised to verbalize the process of cleaning their rifles, as, for example:

First: Pick up the rifle, pull operating mechanism to the rear, and inspect for safety.

Second: Depress follower and follower slide; allow the bolt to close, leaving the rifle cocked.

(And so on, through the other procedures.)

Verbalizing strengthens the memory for motor and mechanical operations.

For the acquiring of information, sight and hearing are the most important senses. But blind people have to learn and remember with their ears and sense of touch. Deaf people must rely largely upon sight. Certain people with normal sight for some reason have very poor ability to learn reading and writing by visual methods. There have been cases of boys of good general intelligence who were unable to learn to read and write in school, but who learned quickly when someone guided their hands through the motions of writing words; they learned a word by learning the movements required to write it. Fortunately these "motor types" are rare.

Some people appear to remember best what they see, others what they hear. For a short time educators believed that it would be wise to find out a person's "type"—visual or auditory—before attempting to teach him. Today the general opinion is that it is better to arrange that the senses reinforce each other.

Visual imagery is very strong in young children, but generally becomes weaker after the age of fourteen. This special ability of children and a few adults is called "eidetic imagery." A person with a "photographic memory" may be called an eidetic. An example of such a person was John von Neumann, a great mathematician who died in 1956. According to Clay Blair, Jr., writing in Life (February 25, 1957), von Neumann, when eight years old, could memorize the names, addresses, and telephone numbers of a column in a telephone directory "on sight." Von Neumann retained his eidetic ability throughout life, being able to carry on difficult mathematical calculations in his mind.

Floyd Ruch, in his Psychology and Life, tells of a law student with eidetic memory who was charged with cheating on an examination because he had reproduced material verbatim from a textbook. He offered to prove his innocence by duplicating the feat under observation. After five minutes' study of new material he was able to write down four hundred words of it exactly as printed.[1]

You are most likely not an eidetic. You might, however, like to know whether you are a visual or an auditory learner or, as is most common, both. You might be able to decide by asking yourself whether you would prefer to learn the contents of an article by reading it or by listening to it delivered as a lecture. You might even test yourself, with someone's assistance, in this way: Have the other person pick out a paragraph of 50-100 words and another passage of the same length and about the same difficulty. Memorize the first paragraph by the process of reading silently the entire paragraph, reciting what you can remember of it, reading it again, reciting, and so on, recording the number of readings necessary for one perfect recitation. Then have the other person read the second passage to you, recite, have him read it again, recite, and so on, recording, as before, the number of readings necessary for one perfect recitation. Compare the results and make your own interpretation.

F. C. Bartlett, after careful studies of visual and auditory memorizers, characterized them as follows:[2]

Visualizers tend to learn rapidly and confidently and also to be confident in reproducing what they have learned. They tend to deal directly with the subject matter, visualizing it as presented and depending less on grouping, comparisons, or secondary associations than auditory memorizers. But Bartlett found that visualizers change the material more, in recalling it, than they realize. They sometimes get the order of things mixed up and sometimes introduce extraneous material. Their attitude is, as a rule, one of confidence, irrespective of objective accuracy.

Auditory memorizers tend to grasp signs or cues and fix them with descriptions. They use classifications, associations, and comparisons more than visualizers do. In recall they tend to respond with some uncertainty even when their memory is accurate.

If you find that you are either strongly visual or strongly auditory, you would do well to realize the weaknesses of your type and to try to strengthen your visual or auditory learning ability, whichever is weaker.

Utilizing both sight and hearing is advantageous in all studies. Names, technical terms, and the words of a foreign language can be learned best if you see and hear them. If you only see them, you lose the value of knowing them in two ways, which reinforce each other. If you know them only as sounds, there is the same loss of double learning, and you have trouble with spelling. In learning names, terms, and foreign words, see and say.

When it comes to facts and ideas, it really does not matter whether you arrive at an understanding of them and impress them on your memory through sight or hearing, though using both is desirable. But an auditory learner should spend more time in reciting orally what he is learning than a visualizer; and, though oral reading is slow, he might do well to read aloud passages he finds difficult. A visualizer probably should take fuller notes on a lecture than an auditory learner.

Visual Aids. Textbooks—as well as newspapers, magazines, and books for the general public—often make use of what are called "visual aids" (maps, charts, diagrams, and illustrations of various kinds) because "a picture is worth a thousand words" and because a large amount of information can be put into an illustration which otherwise would be a great chunk of indigestible print. The most complicated scientific and historical data can be made clear by a diagram. The results of an experiment the description of which takes pages of print can be put in a chart or graph. No business could operate without organizational charts, and graphs showing expenditures, sales, profits, and the like. A newspaper cartoon can set forth a situation (from a certain point of view) more clearly and effectively than a long editorial.

The utilization of visual aids requires a background of information and understanding as regards the subject matter (a person who had never studied chemistry would not be able to understand a chart showing the arrangement of atoms in a protein molecule) and an understanding of the illustrative device used (a child or an illiterate peasant would not understand a pie chart). But a student or reader, it is assumed, finds a visual aid associated with material that he is capable of comprehending. And the interpretation of various standard forms of visual aids is a skill that is acquired as an adjunct to reading.

In studying a textbook you should take full advantage of whatever visual aids may be offered. Too often a student who studies as a duty rather than as a pleasure feels that all that can be expected of him is to read the text and that illustrations, if not interesting, can be skipped. He does not realize that if mastery of the subject is his aim, visual aids are time-savers. One way to fail to benefit from visual aids, then, is the simple one of not paying attention to them. Another reason for failing to utilize these devices is not to understand the "rules of the game" of the various kinds, such as the bar graph, the pie chart, and the statistical curve. Each kind of visual aid is fairly easy to understand if sufficient attention is paid to it. Furthermore, it is necessary to look at and understand every single notation or statement associated with the illustration. Students often fail to understand the significance of the facts represented just because they lack the interest and the patience to give the illustration the careful study it deserves.

If you find that you do not understand a particular illustration (and you do understand the text it illustrates), your failure to understand the illustration is very likely because you have not read, or read carefully, all the explanatory matter. If you are satisfied that you have made as much of an effort as can be expected and still do not understand the thing, ask your instructor to explain it to you.

You might occasionally make your own visual aids. Mark Twain had difficulty remembering his lectures. First, he used a list of topics, or key phrases; but the results were not satisfactory. Then he put minute notations on his fingernails, but it was embarrassing to have to look at his fingernails frequently before an audience. Finally he drew a series of pictures, each on a piece of paper, to illustrate the points of a lecture, and this proved the best memory device. Many years later he could remember the pictures he had drawn and, with them, his lectures.

When you make a diagram to help you remember something, it serves several purposes: you clarify certain facts by simplifying them and arranging them logically; you make sure that you understand the facts, since it is necessary to do so if you are to draw the diagram; you absorb the information in more than one way and thus reinforce it in the memory; you heighten your interest in the subject matter through ego involvement, doing something creative with the facts.

Here is an example from the field of geography. It is very difficult, even after studying maps, to get a clear idea of the relative positions of the nations of the Near East. If you would draw, from a map, a crudely simplified picture of these states (see illustration on page 80), then try to draw it again from memory, compare it with your original picture, draw it again, compare, and so on, until you have no trouble getting the countries in the right places, you would no doubt remember for the rest of your life the arrangement of these countries.

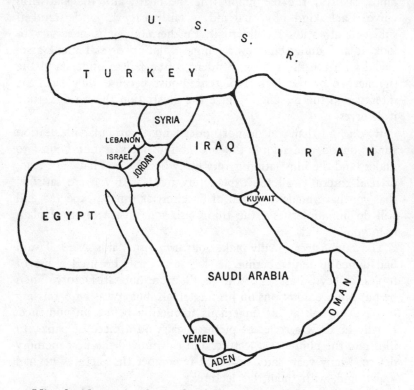

Visual aids as simple as the following can be used. The three basic divisions of the American government are the executive, the legislative, and the judiciary. These can be remembered with the aid of a triangle the sides of which are labeled:

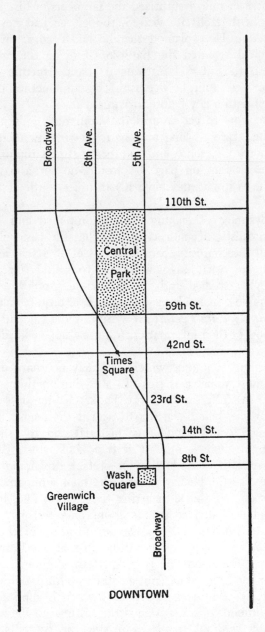

An American tourist surprised the members of his group by his familiarity with each city visited, though he had never been to Europe before. He explained that he had been a traveling salesman and had acquired the habit of studying the map of each city he was to visit and learning its basic structure or pattern. On his European tour, he was using the same method of acquainting himself with a city before arriving at it.

To learn how to get around in Manhattan, it is necessary to picture the island as long and narrow, with numbered avenues running north and south and numbered streets running east and west. The diagram on page 81 would do for a basic pattern, though the visitor would have his troubles south of Fourteenth Street.

The advantage of making such a simplified and (as regards shape) unrealistic diagram as ours is that the basic plan appears without all the confusing complications of an actual map.

To sum up, visual aids you find in your study material are to be thoroughly studied and are invaluable. And the practice of making simple visual aids of your own is also quite valuable.

Efficient Reading Techniques. Since older students and adults acquire most of their information from reading, good silent-reading habits are extremely important.

One reading technique which you may not have utilized and which is most valuable is this: In studying anything but fiction or poetry, carefully examine the book, chapter or section of a book, or article, before starting to read it thoroughly. See how it is organized. Read introductory material and the summary, or conclusion, if there is one. If it is a book, study the table of contents; read the introduction or preface explaining the nature and purpose of the book; and read the final summarizing chapter if there is one. If you are starting the chapter of a book, or an article, and it is divided into sections and perhaps subsections, study the organization. Keep the organization of the whole in mind as you read, so that you will be able, as you learn particular things, to fit them into the larger pattern of thought.

Another good procedure (not a substitute for preliminary examination but an additional procedure), which is applicable to anything you intend to read at one sitting, is to read the whole thing very rapidly, without trying to master the contents. This will give you a general idea of the material you want to learn. Then reread thoroughly, paying special attention to details and difficult passages.

Habits carried over from your early school days, when you read orally and had trouble recognizing and pronouncing words, prevent efficient silent reading unless you get rid of them. These habits are: (1) looking at words one at a time and (2) thinking of the sound of words as you read. To read efficiently you must read by phrases. If you once learned to recognize at a glance words like *thorough, understand,* and *impenetrable,* you can extend your ability to recognize larger wholes and take in at a glance phrases like *in the afternoon, on the other hand,* and *eighteenth century philosophers.*

People who read one word at a time tend to lose track of the thought because it takes them so long to get through the sentence and because they pay attention to the separate words.

But people who read by phrases are able to grasp ideas quickly; their speed of reading approaches the speed of thought.

If you have the common habit of pronouncing words to yourself as you read, you are a word-by-word reader, and your speed of reading is slowed down to your speed of talking. So try to take in ideas without depending upon the childish habit of pronouncing as you read. Read ideas, not words.

People who take courses in what is called "developmental reading" (to distinguish it from "remedial reading") on the average double their reading speed and at the same time improve their comprehension. Many such courses use mechanical aids to push people along and force them to break the pronouncing and one-word-at-a-time habits. But anyone who realizes that efficient silent reading means breaking these habits can, by effort and practice, improve his reading speed and his comprehension.

It is not true that slow readers understand what they read better than rapid readers; in fact, the opposite is generally true (within limits, of course).

Finally, you should adapt your reading speed and reading methods to your purpose and the difficulty of the material. If the material is easy to understand and not important to you, you should read it very rapidly or skim it. Difficult material that you want to understand thoroughly and remember requires slower reading, even rereading—but this does not mean word-by-word reading.

Writing as an Aid to Learning. The word "writing" in the title of this section includes all use of pen or pencil for learning purposes.

You may remember meeting this statement before; it is still true: A judicious use of pen or pencil as you read a book is a valuable study technique. At this time we shall consider more fully the "judicious use of pen or pencil."

N. B. The advice that follows applies only to reading material that you own.

Some of the old feeling that what is printed is sacred still remains with us. It is good to respect a book, but it is foolish to be afraid or ashamed to write in a book or make useful marks in it. Books are tools. You can make them more useful to you, now and in the future, by marking them in various ways.

There are two advantages to marking a book that do not come from referring to the markings later. The first is that marking gives you more of a feeling of identification with the book. By marking it, you bring it down off its pedestal and make it to a fuller extent your own book. Furthermore, when you make the book more useful to you by marking it and give added emphasis to what is important in it, you have a feeling of cooperating to a small extent with the author.

Another and very important advantage of marking your book is that to mark what is important or what is difficult requires you to be mentally alert so as to pick out the important and the difficult things. Therefore marking your book makes you a better reader, an active rather than a passive reader.

Now there are many ways of marking books. Some suggestions follow, but use what you like and what seems most useful to you.

Textbooks use center and/or side headings to indicate divisions and subdivisions of a chapter. If you are studying a book whose chapters are not subdivided, you can write your own heading in the margin whenever a new topic is begun.

You might use a red pencil to underline or encircle such small items as a date to be remembered, an important name (when first mentioned), or a technical term (when first defined or used). If you do not care to use a red pencil to encircle these occasional items, an asterisk will make them stand out from the underlined passages.

If you get the underlining habit, you must guard against over-doing it. Underlining too much is like using strong language too much—it loses its effect when not used in moderation.

One underlining system is to underline topic sentences. In expository prose, as a rule about two-thirds of the paragraphs begin with a topic sentence, the sentence that contains the main thought of the paragraph. In other paragraphs the topic sentence may be the second one or the last one or somewhere in between, and sometimes there is no topic sentence. The chief defect of this method is that sometimes a topic sentence announces a topic but does not really say anything about it. Often there are very important statements that are not topic sentences. So merely underlining topic sentences is somewhat too rigid a system. But it has the virtue of keeping your eye on the ball. The suggestion is to underline topic sentences (with a few exceptions, such as those in short and unimportant paragraphs) and also other important statements.

Now what would be a good use of underlining in the preceding paragraph? The topic sentence comes first and should be under-lined. If you have forgotten what a topic sentence is and think you may need a reminder, underline the latter part of the second sentence, which defines a topic sentence. The paragraph contains a criticism of the system; so you might underline the sentence beginning with "Often"—or just underline "Often . . . important statements . . . are not topic sentences." The paragraph ends with a recommendation, part of which deserves underlining: "underline topic sentences . . . and also other important statements." (You need not always underline an entire sentence; you can well leave out relatively unimportant phrases and clauses.) If you read the whole paragraph before underlining anything, you will see that to underline the first sentence and the final words, "and also other important statements," would be sufficient.

A minimum use of underlining would be to underline only important statements that you think you might forget. Or you might just underline a few phrases to serve as cues. How much to underline should be learned by experience.

An alternative to underlining is to put a vertical line in the margin alongside an important passage, with perhaps two lines for something of special importance. A big star in the margin would serve the same purpose, perhaps with a bracket to show what lines it calls attention to.

It is a good idea to put a question mark in the margin to indicate something that you doubt or do not understand. An exclama tion mark can call attention to something astonishing. This leads to the area of self-expression. You can put comments in the margin, even impolite ones, give the author an argument, or supplement his discussion of a topic if you like—it is your book and marking it or writing in it sensibly is making good use of it.

You may not own the book you are studying. If you are to be tested on it or want to retain the information for personal reasons, you will have to take notes on it.

It is important to write your notes legibly and neatly, so that you will not give up in disgust when you look at them later. Notes should be not too scanty and not too full—just sufficient to set forth clearly the ideas and facts that you want to remember. It is a waste of time and effort to write fully expressed sentences. Nor should phrases be so brief as to be uncommunicative.

Suppose that you have borrowed this book and are taking notes on it. If you feel that you do not need the advice given in the preceding paragraph, make no notes on it. If you want to take some notes, you might write:

> Notes on books:
>   Legible and neat.
>   Note only ideas and facts to be remembered.
>   Phrases not too brief—should express idea clearly.

Your notes should indicate clearly the organization of the book. Include chapter and section titles; use capitals for chapter titles and underline section titles.

In reviewing notes which you expect to review again, you might mark in some way the things difficult to remember, so that in the next review you can concentrate on what you need to review.

Taking notes on a lecture is more difficult. Since the lecturer goes right on talking, you have to use the utmost economy in jotting down the most important ideas and facts. Unless you are very skillful at the job, you would do well to rewrite your notes as soon as possible, filling in what is necessary from memory while your memory is fresh.

Remember, marking up your books and taking notes on lectures serve two purposes: (1) to keep you mentally alert as you read or listen, and (2) to assist you in reviewing.

Recitation (Self-testing). Perhaps you think of reciting as something done in the classroom, as evidence for the teacher that you have learned your assignment. But we are here considering the kind of reciting in which you are the student and the teacher; you recite to yourself to see whether you should say to yourself "Well done!" or "Back to work!"

There is one kind of learning in which everyone, even a young child, feels the necessity for self-testing, and that is memorizing something—a poem, a speech, or lines for a play. This situation seems to carry with it the realization that the thing is either learned or not learned and that recitation is the only way to find out when learning is completed.

Another kind of learning task in which many students recite to themselves (and all should) is the learning of vocabulary in a foreign-language course. This, too, is memorizing, but the task is quite different from the learning of a piece of literature. It is a matter of linking each foreign word with its English equivalent and, to complete the process, linking each English word with its foreign equivalent. (For self-testing, it is necessary to make two separate lists, one of foreign words and one of English words.)

Recitation serves to let the learner know when his task is completed. It saves time and effort because it reveals just where more study is required. And it promotes faster learning because it is a more active process than listening or reading. Furthermore, recitation leads to the detection and correction of mistakes.

Arthur I. Gates carried on an experiment with eighth-grade children in the memorizing of nonsense syllables, which demonstrates the advantage of reciting.[3] Here are his findings:

Per Cent of Time Spent Reading	Per Cent of Time Spent Reciting	Average Number of Syllables Remembered
100	0	65.4
80	20	92.2
60	40	99.7
40	60	105.5
20	80	137.3

Later experiments have indicated that the advantage of recitation in the memorizing of meaningful material is somewhat less than that with Gates' nonsense syllables, but it is still an advantage. And even if there were no advantage in speed, recitation would be necessary for the discovery and correction of errors and for knowing when the learning job was done.

Now what about the value of reciting, or self-testing, when the learning task is not one of memorizing? The arguments for self-testing apply to any kind of task. But how should you go about testing yourself on a chapter of a textbook or an article from a magazine?

First, you can ask yourself: Am I satisfied with my understanding of what I have read? Is it all perfectly clear, or are there some things that are a bit hazy? If you are dissatisfied with your understanding and recollection of the material, are you unsure of the whole thing, or just of some parts? And what parts need further study?

Another approach is to put yourself in the teacher's place: if you had given this assignment to a class, what would you consider important, what questions would you ask, what kind of a written test would you give? If your chapter has eight sections, you might consider that a fair test would require an understanding of the central thought of each section. You can turn the heading of any section into a question and see whether you can give a clear and correct answer to that question. For example (from English history text): Heading: "Babington's Plot"—Question: "What was Babington's plot?" Some headings would suggest a number of questions; as Heading: "The Battle of Poitiers"—Questions: "When did the battle of Poitiers take place? Where is Poitiers? Who fought? Who won? What was the significance of the battle?"

If you want to test yourself objectively and honestly, write down your list of topics ("Babington's plot," etc.). For if you look at the heading in the book, you can hardly avoid seeing certain names, dates, or words that give you cues, and if you hold the book open you will probably glance at it when you have trouble reciting.

In reciting do not parrot the words of the text; if you understand the subject you can put it into your own words.

It would be most effective to recite on each section of the assignment immediately after studying it and then once more on each section after studying the whole assignment.

You can prepare the way for recitation ahead of time by

underlining or otherwise marking, as you read, things you feel you should remember.

Benjamin Franklin made good use of recitation of an unusual kind. As a youth he wished to improve his writing ability. He came upon a volume of the *Spectator* papers and greatly admired the style of these essays (most of them the work of Addison and Steele). He decided to model his own style upon them but soon realized the ineffectiveness of merely reading and imitating them. So he hit upon this device: He would jot down as briefly as possible the thought of each sentence in an essay and, several days later, would rewrite the essay from his notes in imitation of the style of the original. Then, comparing his essay with the original, he would note his faults, his stylistic limitations, and the meagerness of his vocabulary. Stuart P. Sherman, in the *Cambridge History of American Literature*, says of Franklin's style: "It is the flexible style of a writer who has learned the craft of expression by studying and imitating the virtues of many masters."[4] Like Franklin, you should adapt the technique of recitation to your needs and purposes; if the common kinds of recitation do not serve, use your ingenuity and devise another kind.

Review and Use. The curve of forgetting, as has already been remarked, has the same shape as the apparatus down which children slide in the park. Forgetting gets under way with a zoom and then slows down continuously as time goes on. The best time to review is, therefore, soon after learning has taken place.

The Roman statesman Cato must have realized this fact, for he formed the habit of sitting down in the evening, before he went to bed, and recalling everything worthy of review in the day's events. Napoleon III used a similar technique; as soon as he found himself alone after an audience, he would write down and review the names of the persons he had talked with. When John Quincy Adams was thirteen years old, he began his lifelong habit of carefully recording in his diary the details about everything of importance. His memory for this information was remarkable—a testimony, in part at least, to the value of prompt review.

Students will do well to review a lesson in the evening of the same day that they have attended a class studying the lesson.

In reviewing it would be wise to take into consideration the fact that material at the beginning and at the end is best remembered and that material in the middle is most likely to be forgotten. In such a standard memory experiment as learning nonsense syllables it is found that the syllables first learned are those at the beginning and end, and learning proceeds inward toward the middle. The peak of difficulty is just beyond the middle toward the end. The midparts of a learning task need the most practice.

In some kinds of learning (as memorizing) there would be a disadvantage in changing the method of review. But with other kinds of learning there might be an advantage in changing the method. This can be illustrated by an example from advertisement-testing. It has been found that an advertisement gets more attention and is remembered better if it is slightly varied on each presentation than if it is shown in identical form the same number of times. This would suggest that review is more effective if done with thoughtful consideration each time and if the material is examined for various meanings and from different points of view.

The best review is use. A good example is the learning of foreign-language vocabulary. After you have learned your new words one at a time and have recited them, you go on to translate sentences from the other language into English and vice versa. This practice in using the word establishes it in your memory.

Sometimes, however, no occasion for use arises. Many matters are set forth once in a book and not referred to again. Then the original learning must be reinforced by review without use.

In studying a textbook it is a valuable procedure to review the unit last studied before tackling the new unit.*

Spaced Practice. The value of spaced practice has been well proved by a number of experiments. In one of them Piéron required a subject to memorize series of twenty digits. When the digits were repeated with thirty-second intervals, eleven repetitions were necessary for one correct recitation. When the digits were repeated at five-minute intervals, only six repetitions were required. With ten-minute intervals, five repetitions sufficed.[5]

Of course, as the interval between periods of learning, or reviewing, is increased, a point of diminishing gains is reached. The best spacing for practice of a particular subject would depend upon the nature and extent of the task and would have to be guessed at. But the principle is that spacing practice promotes learning

---

* For helpful suggestions on studying textbooks, see *Best Methods of Study*, in the College Outline Series, published by Barnes & Noble, Inc.

unless the interval is so long that forgetting takes place. A practical application would be: If you can spend two hours mastering a unit of a subject, you would not do well to put in the two hours at one sitting because fatigue would set in and attention would slacken. It would be better to work for an hour, or to complete one thorough reading; then after the lapse of an hour or two (preferably not spent on mental labor, and certainly not on a similar task) to review the material. Probably two spaced half-hours or three spaced twenty-minute periods would be more effective than an hour of reviewing and reciting. In this as in everything else, use your own judgment.

The more meaningful and interesting the subject, the less need for spaced practice. Spaced practice is most useful in memorizing tasks.

Spaced practice has an added value. It has been discovered that unfinished tasks are remembered better than finished tasks. (Glance back at Chapter IV, "Forgetting by Completing," page 45.) B. Zeigarnik gave a group of people twenty tasks, ten of which he allowed them to complete. Each of the other ten tasks was removed with the remark, "That is enough now; turn to this other task." At the end the subjects were asked to list as many tasks as they could remember. The average percentages for tasks remembered were: unfinished tasks, 68 per cent; finished tasks, 42 per cent.[6]

Kurt Lewin conducted a somewhat similar experiment and found 90 per cent better recall for unfinished than for finished tasks. He inferred that leaving a task unfinished created a state of tension.[7]

The practical significance of the facts just presented is that one would do well to begin a learning task even if there is not time to complete it until a later occasion.

The opposite of spaced practice is "cramming." Here and now I shall only say that it is an inefficient practice.

Sleeping Over It. Sleep that "knits up the raveled sleeve of care" will not knit up your raveled memories, but neither will it unravel them to any extent.

Ebbinghaus, constructing his curves of forgetting, found, in testing recall after various periods, a certain irregularity in the results: an unexpectedly small difference between recall after eight hours and after fifteen hours. We now know that this irregularity was due to the different effect on forgetting between elapsed daytime hours and elapsed hours partly spent in sleep.

Jenkins and Dallenbach, as has been mentioned in Chapter IV, found that freshly learned material was remembered much better after a period of sleep than after an equal period of daytime activity. The reason is obvious: daytime mental activity creates interference.

Woodworth, in his *Psychology*, cites two subsequent studies of the problem:[8] R. Heine tested recall for material memorized early in the evening and just before going to bed. She found about ten per cent difference in favor of learning just before sleeping. J. B. Spight investigated the question, is it better to start memorizing a piece in the evening and finish it in the morning, or vice versa? He found an advantage of ten per cent for beginning in the evening and finishing in the morning.

Therefore, in learning something on which you are to be tested the next day, it would be best to learn it in the evening just before bedtime and review it the next day shortly before the test.

There is, however, the factor of fatigue. H. P. Maity found, using tests of immediate recall, that during the course of the day memorizing became increasingly difficult.[9] Therefore the advice should be modified: study before going to bed *unless* you are physically or mentally overtired.

It is assumed that the amount of learning or reviewing is moderate; the foregoing advice is not to be taken as suggesting cramming.

Overlearning. The steepness of the typical curve of forgetting is partially due to the fact that in a learning experiment one or two perfect recitations are considered evidence of learning. For practical purposes this degree of learning is insufficient. People generally realize this fact, for in memorizing something that is to be recited before an audience, in learning a song, a speech, or the lines of a play, they go on reviewing and reciting as often as time permits. Reviewing something that has already been learned sufficiently for one perfect recitation is called *overlearning*, and the only way to be confident of being able to recall a thing is to overlearn it. The prefix *over-* usually means "too much"—but not in this instance.

Everything you can recall without effort has been overlearned through frequent use. Some things, such as your name, have been overlearned through use far more than necessary. The necessity for intentional overlearning exists with knowledge that is not going to be used frequently.

Ebbinghaus conducted an experiment that shows the results of overlearning.[10] He found that he could learn a set of nonsense syllables sufficiently for one perfect recitation in eight readings. After a certain period of time he relearned the list and found a saving, in time, of 8 per cent. The following table shows the increased retention with a larger number of readings:

No. of Readings	Per Cent of Savings in Relearning
8	8
16	15
24	23
32	33
64	64

The consistency of the relation between number of readings and retention suggests the probability that with a hundred readings, retention would be excellent.

The only rule to follow in learning something that will not be frequently used is to overlearn it as much as possible—as long as you have any doubt of your ability to recall it when you want it. The more important and the more difficult the thing, the more you should reinforce it with practice. It is of course impossible to overlearn everything you would like to remember, so you have to select certain things for overlearning, realizing that a thing is not really learned unless it is overlearned.

Overlearning in some instances can be a waste of time. If a student of a foreign language makes long lists of words and repeats each word until he knows them all, he will spend too much time on the easy words and too little on the hard words. When studying German I found that I learned some words with only two repetitions, while others had to be practiced fourteen times to be learned. Using the card system (a card for each word) enables one to give just the right amount of overlearning to each word.

Finding a Principle or Pattern. Things to be learned are so various that learning requires a great variety of methods. The basic principles of learning discussed in Chapter V apply, of course, to learning in general. And the study methods we have been considering apply to study in general. But the specific thing to be learned often requires a specific method.

In learning miscellaneous small items of knowledge it is important to look for a principle, or pattern, by which to remember a certain thing. Here are a few illustrations of finding a principle or pattern:

(1) The spelling of *Mississippi* is very easy once you have noted the pattern: M-i-ss-i-ss-i-pp-i, that is, after initial *M* there are *i*'s alternating with double letters. The spelling of *dining* (sometimes spelt *dineing* or *dinning* by students) requires knowledge and application of a principle—drop -e before -ing—and the nonapplication of a principle that does not apply.

(2) If you need to remember a certain number, you may be able to see a pattern in it: for example, 27496 contains two patterns, 2-4-6 and -7-9-. The patterns that can be seen in numbers (including, of course, addresses and telephone numbers) are numerous and varied.

(3) In learning to recognize a person, you need to look for a pattern of individual features in all the different appearances of the person as he sits, stands, walks, talks, listens, smiles, frowns, and so on, and appears in various locations and in various costumes.

(4) In learning a piece of music it is necessary to see, underlying the peculiarities of each passage, the rhythmic and melodic patterns of the whole.

(5) In studying the customs of a tribe or other group of people, it is necessary to look for a principle or pattern that unifies a number of customs or beliefs—such as cooperativeness or acquisitive rivalry.

(6) In studying the inflections of a foreign language you find certain patterns of endings repeated, each time with a variation characteristic of the tense or mood. Thus, to look at only the first person plural, present active, of three typical Spanish verbs: we have:

> from *hablar: hablamos*
> *deber: debemos*
> *partir: partimos*

And in other tenses of *hablar* we find the same pattern:

Present: hablamos
Imperfect: hablábamos
Future: hablaremos

The student soon realizes that the ending -mos is part of a pat
tern of personal endings; he learns this pattern and combines it
with other patterns for the various tenses and moods.

Sometimes the pattern is given and explained by teacher or
textbook; sometimes the pattern is obvious; but often the pattern
must be searched for. Sometimes, as with the rules of spelling,
grammar, and punctuation, it is a difficult task to remember all
the principles and patterns that must be applied to individual
cases.

CHAPTER VII

Some Memory Devices and Systems

Nearly all memory systems were developed before the days of printing. In all the systems something has been added to the material. Sometimes the addition is an encumbrance and almost overwhelms the thing one wishes to recall.

Some of the simpler devices are very useful. Certain complicated systems have been, and still are being, demonstrated in public performances (often quite remarkable) and sold in the form of courses and books, and many people have given fervid testimonials to their value. Professional memory experts who demonstrate these systems specialize in certain feats which are somewhat like a magician's tricks; they are based on the skilled use of a system for a particular situation. The memory experts do not seem to have remarkable memories for all kinds of subject matter and all kinds of situations.

Francis Bacon asserted, in *De Augmentis Scientiarum*, that in elaborate memory systems the attention is misdirected by, and consumed with, the accessories of memorizing at the expense of solid understanding; they are, he said, like "rope dancing, antic postures, and feats of activity, . . . the one being the abuse of the bodily as the other is of the mental powers, and though they cause admiration [wonder], they cannot be highly esteemed."[1]

I do not wish to wholly condemn the commercialized memory systems. They may be very useful to some individuals who can apply the system to their own vocations and needs.

Rhymes. Before writing was invented, all the kinds of knowledge that we preserve in books had to be preserved in the memories of certain people who specialized in learning and teaching the lore of the tribe. Because it is easier to remember rhythmical than unrhythmical material and because emotion tends to be expressed in rhythmical form, most primitive history, science, magic and religion, literature, and other folklore took the form of poetry. The memory value of rhythm was reinforced with music and dancing.

Rhyme is a relatively modern invention; it originated—so it is generally believed—in Catholic ceremonials, the device of rhyme having been invented by priests to assist the populace in learning songs and responses.

We are all familiar with a few rhymes that help us to remember, and probably all of us rely on "Thirty days hath September, April, June, and November."

Of unquestionable value for children and adults who cannot remember when to use *ie* and *ei* in spelling is the old verse:

> *I* before *e*
> Except after c,
> Or when sounded like a,
> As in *neighbor* or *weigh*.

Such rhymes are not used in education today as much as formerly. But even a professor of philosophy may occasionally resort to the device to make a point, as when he recites the well-known little verse about the centipede that fell into a ditch because the ant asked him, "Pray, which leg comes after which?"—or the unrhymed but rhythmical aphorism, "What is mind? No matter. What is matter? Never mind."

Although the device of putting information into verse has fallen into disuse, if you are very clever at versifying you might make your own rhymes, such as:

> Garden 6—1242
> Is the number of my friend Lou.

If the number is Sally's:

> For Sally nothing else will do
> But Garden 6—1242.

Or if it is Joe Wally's number:

> To get Joe Wally, this I do:
> Dial Garden 6—1242.

What if you want to remember Mr. Higgintwoffle's number, Albermarle 7—6915? Well:

> Higgintwoffle comes alive
> With Al 7—6915.

Here is one more:

> Sophie McGinty's not in Heaven;
> Call Circle 3—4157.

Memory devices do not have to meet rigorous logical or esthetic standards. For example:

> Pavlov, dogs: conditionism—
> Watson and behaviorism.

This feeble verse, using the nonexistent term "conditionism" and a deplorable rhyme, can still serve to remind you that the behaviorist school of psychology, in which John B. Watson was the leading figure, was based upon the fact of conditioning, discovered by Pavlov in his experiments with dogs.

Numbering. It is very difficult to learn anything if the parts are not learned in a certain order. Imagine a child trying to learn the alphabet by naming the letters at random as they occur to him—"l u f y . . . ," "s c o a . . .," "b w i t . . . ," and so on. The value of order is enhanced by numbering.

In the Biblical book of *Exodus* there is a famous passage that begins:

And God spoke all these words, saying, "I am the Lord thy God, which have brought thee out of the land of Egypt, out of the house of bondage. "Thou shalt have no other gods before me. . . ."

For many, many centuries Hebrews and, later, Christians felt it imperative for their children to learn this Scriptural passage. For the facilitation of learning and remembering and of reference, the series of divine prohibitions came to be called the "Ten Commandments."

H. G. Wells, writing of Gautama Buddha in his *Outline of History,* says:

The master . . . worked out and composed pithy and brief verses, aphorisms, and lists of "points," and these were expounded in the discourse of his disciples. It greatly helped them to have these points and aphorisms numbered. The modern mind is apt to be impatient of the tendency of Indian thought to a numerical statement of things, the Eightfold Path, the Four Truths, and so on, but this enumeration was a mnemonic necessity in an undocumented world.[2]

Numbering has not lost its value, as Wells implies; it has the same value for us as for Buddha's disciples. If you should want to learn the eight principles of righteousness called the "Eightfold Path," you would find it more difficult to learn them unnumbered than as "1, Right doctrine; 2, Right purpose"; and so on.

The great advantage of numbering is that, besides enforcing order, it serves as a check. If you name ten Commandments, you know that you have named them all.

Numbering is very useful for learning any classification, or series, of from three to fifteen or twenty members. One example from science: knowing that there are six geologic eras (from Azoic to Cenozoic) is a great advantage to one learning these rather strange-appearing terms for the first time. Students of government and law must learn the Amendments to the Constitution by their numbers.

With large numbers of items, numbering loses its value. Unless for some very special purpose, there would be no value in learning the fifty states by giving each a number. (If for some reason you did want to memorize the names of the states so that you could run through them rapidly, you could do so by grouping them in ten groups of five or five groups of ten.) The hundred or so chemical elements could be learned in the same way.

Alphabetical Order. Sometimes putting things into alphabetical order helps. It is one way of imposing order upon a set of items that provide no basis for logical order. If you wanted to memorize the fifty states, you would find the job easier if you alphabetized them: "Alabama Alaska Arizona Arkansas, California Colorado Connecticut"; and so on. In this way each item provides a cue for the next item. You would soon learn that there are four A's, no B's, three C's, one D, no E's, and so on.

The alphabet may be used in searching for a lost name or word. Let us say the lost item is the last name of Henry —◡ (you remember that the last name has two syllables, with the accent on the first one). Well, you can ask yourself, does it begin with A? B? C? and so on. Now suppose that you recall that the name begins with W, or you think so. Then try Wa-, We-, Wh-, Wi-,

Wo-, Wr-, Wu-, and Wy-, which seem to be the only possibilities. If you still have not hit upon the name but think you are on the right track with Wh-, then try Wha-, Whe-, Whi-, Who-, Whu-, and Why-. This method does not always work, but it is worth a try. The chief difficulty is being sure of the first letter.

The discussion of "blocking" in Chapter IV, pages 44-45, is relevant here.

Abbreviation. Abbreviation was used by the ancient Greeks and Romans as a time- and parchment-saving device, and was no doubt also used by them as a memory device. Its usefulness is quite obvious.

The essence of abbreviation is the use of a part for the whole. The commonest form of abbreviation is that used with names. For general purposes it is sufficient to remember that *Don Quixote* was written by "Cervantes" (rather than Miguel de Cervantes Saavedra) and that the famous American showman was "Barnum" or "P. T. Barnum" (rather than Phineas Taylor Barnum).

As long names and terms have multiplied, it has become necessary to use more and more abbreviations. Speaking and writing about chemistry would be almost impossible without such abbreviations as H_2SO_4. Consider the usefulness—for reference, printing, and learning—of:

ACTH: adreno-cortico-trophic hormone (hyphens supplied by author)
RAS: reticular activating system (of the brain)

For the same reasons it has become necessary to use abbreviations in referring to well-known political and other organizations. The usual method of abbreviation is just to use the initials of the words composing the name: WPA, CIO, FTC, M. I. T., SPCA, NATO. The great value of abbreviations for learning, as well as reference, is obvious with such long names as:

NSDAP: National Sozialistische Deutsche Arbeiters Partei (NSDAP later largely replaced by "Nazi")
UNESCO: United Nations Educational, Scientific, and Cultural Organization
MOUSE (an acrostic): Minimal Orbital Unmanned Satellite of Earth

You can, of course, not only take advantage of existing abbreviations, but also make your own. For example, if you want to remember James A. Whiffletree's full name, you can remember him as JAW (and it would help if he has a large jaw or is quite a talker). You could remember Charles A. Dimble as CHAD.

Or if you are going to the grocery for bread, milk, cream, peas, carrots, and fish, you might alphabetize them and remember the initials BCC,FMP.

Learning a series of names or terms in their proper order is often facilitated by learning the initials. For example, the names of the planets and their order as regards nearness to the Sun: MVEM, JSUNP. JSUN can be pronounced "Jason," and the whole thing can be said as "M V E M, Jason and Pluto." You must know, of course, that the first M is Mercury and the second M is Mars, but you can remember this by the well-known fact that Mars is relatively near the Earth. You will not be confused by the initials SUN because the list is a list of planets.

One type of abbreviation telescopes words:

Comintern: Communist International
Gestapo: German State Police
Benelux: customs union of Belgium, Netherlands, and Luxembourg
ECOSOC: Economic and Social Council (of the United Nations)

Ideas, as well as names and words, may be abbreviated—by the use of key words or phrases. Learning the Ten Commandments, for example, may be facilitated by memorizing the following phrases and words, which represent whole sentences, or ideas:

1. Other gods	6. Killing
2. Graven images	7. Adultery
3. Name of Lord	8. Stealing
4. Sabbath day	9. False witness
5. Father and mother	10. Coveting

Another example, the "Bill of Rights":

1. Freedom of religion, speech, press, petition
2. Arms
3. Quartering soldiers (or just "Quartering")
4. Search and seizure
5. (A) Indictment
   (B) Double jeopardy
   (C) Self-incrimination
   (D) Legal trial
   (E) Private property
6. Speedy and public trial
7. Suits at common law
8. Bail, fines, punishments
9. Rights not mentioned
10. States' rights

Still another example: An actor taking the part of Jacques in *As You Like It* might learn the long speech on the seven ages of man by memorizing, first:

1. Infant	5. Justice
2. Schoolboy	6. Pantaloon
3. Lover	7. Second childhood
4. Soldier	

The same technique can be applied to the learning of speeches. Suppose a man is planning an after-dinner speech. When the speech is worked out, he finds that he is going to make four points, each tied to a joke. The jokes:

1. A young man was telling his friend about his first date with a new girl friend. "She looked good enough to eat—and, great guns, did she!"
2. The teacher asked Johnny whether he could define *moron*, and he said, "Sure. Girls wouldn't catch cold so much in winter if they had more on."
3. A psychoanalyst was asked to treat a cow that would not give milk. He found out that the animal had a fodder complex.
4. A certain man had a lovely wife and two beautiful daughters, but he was very unhappy. He complained that his salary ran into only three figures.

The speaker-to-be attempts to keep the four parts of his speech in mind by means of four words in numerical order: (1) date, (2) moron, (3) cow, (4) figures. A logical organization of ideas might be preferable, but this system would be helpful—and perhaps the speech is not logical.

There are two objections to the use of abbreviations: (1) People sometimes learn an abbreviation and stop there, without learning what it stands for (ACTH, Nazi). (2) Sometimes abbreviations create confusion (UNESCO is sometimes erroneously taken to mean "United Nations Economic and Social Council"—which is ECOSOC).

Acrostics. The word *acrostic* is used loosely here and will be defined by examples.

The word FACE has long been used by music teachers to make it easy for children to remember the notes between the lines on the treble clef. It is not a typical acrostic, however, because the letters do not stand for words.

NATO and "Jason" (for JSUN: Jupiter, Saturn, Uranus, Neptune) are examples of making a word, either a real word or something pronounceable, from the initials of a name or a series of names. Here are some other examples:

MACEY: Marie, Antoinette, Cecile, Emile, Yvonne—the Dionne quintuplets

ROY G. BIV: red, orange, yellow, green, blue, indigo, violet—the colors of the spectrum

PODSCORB: planning, organizing, directing, staffing, coordinating, reporting, budgeting—the major functions of administration. (This word was manufactured by Dr. Arthur H. Gulick, former City Administrator for New York City.)

In another kind of acrostic, when the initials are unpronounceable, they are used to form new words that make a sentence. When a music teacher teaches a beginner the notes of the treble clef, he uses the sentence "Every Good Boy Does Fine (or Deserves Fun)" to help the child remember the notes on the lines: EGBDF.

Medical students have long learned the cranial nerves by the rhyme "On Old Olympus' Tiny Top A Finn And German Viewed Some Hops," the nerves represented by the first letter of each word being: olfactory, optic, oculomotor, trochlear, trigeminal, abducens, facial, auditory, glossopharyngeal, vagus, spinal accessory, and hypoglossal.

Usually people have to be given an acrostic. But a clever person can invent his own when the situation calls for one. A student of biology devised the following: Kings Play Cards On Fairly Good Soft Velvet, for kingdom, phylum, class, order, family, genus, species, variety.

Here is an example of solving a problem by using ingenuity: During World War II a young man was appointed paymaster of a naval vessel. Regulations forbid a paymaster to write down the combination of the safe or to share knowledge of it with anyone. But the paymaster has the privilege of selecting the combination. After thinking over the matter very carefully, the young man chose his wife's first name and the date of her birthday to provide the letters and numbers for the safe's combination. He reasoned that if he forgot his wife's name and birthday there would be no use in his coming home.

Between 1889 and 1913 the departments of the United States

Government were sometimes taught with the aid of the acrostic ST. WAPNIAC. When the Department of Labor was established, it became necessary to use "ST. WAPNIAC + L." But this acrostic would no longer serve when the Departments of War and Navy were consolidated in the Department of Defense and the Department of Health, Education, and Welfare was created. But there are a number of possibilities for a new acrostic, since the order in which the departments are named is not important. In place of useless old St. Wapniac, we can create ST. CHAP-LAID, or ST. LADICHAP, or ST. HADICLAP, or ST. ALPHA-CID, or a more worldly character, DIC ASPHALT. Anagrams are fun.

Would you like to exercise your ingenuity? If so, try to make an acrostic from the names of the presidents of the United States in the twentieth century: Roosevelt, Taft, Wilson, Harding, Coolidge, Hoover, Roosevelt, Truman, Eisenhower . . . .

An acrostic, like some other devices, has the value that it serves to let you know when you have learned or remembered all the items.

The acrostic device is open to criticism. An eminent writer once told me that as a boy he had trouble remembering the spelling of geography and arithmetic. A teacher taught him the acrostics "George Eliot's old grandmother ran a pig home yesterday" and "A red Indian thought he might eat tobacco in church." Well, he learned to spell geography and arithmetic, but he identified the spelling of the words with the sentences so completely that for the rest of his life he could not spell them without the aid of George Eliot's old grandmother and the red Indian.

Another objection is that the acrostic may, with time and disuse, become altered. "On Old Olympus' Tiny Top" could become "On Old Olympus' Snowy Top." Such a change might cause a serious error if the acrostic is depended upon.

The basic objection to acrostics is that they are artificial and do not improve a person's understanding of the matter in question; in fact, they sometimes lead him to rely on the crutch of the acrostic instead of trying to understand.

Still, for the learning of a long, difficult series of names or terms, they are a very present help in time of need. Many people have, by means of an acrostic, remembered certain things all their lives which they would soon have forgotten otherwise.

Pigeonholing (Spatial Arrangement). The pigeonhole memory system is a venerable device which is said to have originated as a result of an earthquake over twenty-four hundred years ago. Simonides, a poet and rhetorician of the little Aegean island of Ceos, attended a banquet. Fortunately for him, while at the banquet he was called to the gateway of the house on a matter of business. At this moment an earthquake occurred, and the banquet guests were crushed under the stones of the house. The bodies were so mutilated that they were unrecognizable. But Simonides was able to identify them because he remembered the place of each man at the banquet table. Later he realized that he had come upon an important and useful principle of memory: we remember many things by their location. Things that have no location, such as ideas, can be put into an imaginary location.

As a simple illustration, the man referred to not far back, who was to make a speech of four parts, each tied to a joke, could use a square, with a key word in each quarter:

1 date	2 moron
3 cow	4 figures

He would have to remember to use both "upstairs rooms" before coming downstairs. And if he made a practice of using pigeonholes, he should always follow the same order.

With twelve items to be remembered, they could be arranged to go around the dial of a watch (which could conveniently lie on the table in front of the speaker). The dial could be used with fewer than twelve items. This system would work only for a person with vivid visual imagery.

Some four hundred years after Simonides, Cicero used a variation of the Greek's system for memorizing his own orations. Instead of a pigeonhole system, Cicero used the familiar parts of his house and garden. When his speech was fully worked out, he would put the first part of his speech in a certain location and proceed from there to other locations, identifying each part of the speech with a certain location. Then in delivering the speech he would, in imagination, walk through his house and grounds, finding in each new location the next topic he would discuss. One can visualize Cicero actually making the rounds as he memorized his speech.

The Romans called this system *topology* (from the Greek word meaning *place*), and from it came our word *topic*. The expressions "in the first place," "in the second place," and so on are said to have the same origin.

The use of the pigeonhole system has not been limited to public speaking. In fact, it has been recommended more for unorganized items, such as the activities one expects to carry out during the day. Its weakness is that, although it puts things into some order, there may be no logic or reason to this order. It is always better to organize ideas logically than merely to arrange them spatially.

Translation (Numbers-Letters). The method of translation is a way of changing numbers into words or vice versa. It is not certain whether this technique was originated by the great mathematician and philosopher Leibniz or whether he merely made some use of it and commented favorably upon it. He writes of the secret of remembering numbers permanently by representing each number with a particular consonant.

Stanislaus Mink von Wenaussheim, who lived at the same time as Leibniz, is credited with inventing this device of turning numbers into words. The system, improved several times, has continued in use.

Disregarding vowels and operating on the basis of sound (with no distinction between single and double letters), we let the following letters and combinations stand for numbers:

1	2	3	4	5	6	7	8	9	0
d	n	m	r	l	soft g	hard g	t	b	soft c
t					j	k	v	p	s, z
					ch, sh				

With this system we can turn numbers into nonsense syllables, words, or phrases. The number 302,594 becomes "Mason leaper" (or, if one prefers, "Miss Nelly Pry"), as follows: 3 0 2 5 9 4
m s n l p r

The number 3,170,850 will translate into "My dog has fleas":
3 1 7 0 8 5 0
m d g s t l s

Now, to start with a name, Mr. Orr translates into 4. John
Stroud would be 62-0141: J n S t r d
6 2 0 1 4 1

Appointments can be represented by numbers and then be
translated into words or phrases. Thus, an appointment on Wednesday, the fourth day of the week, at three o'clock would become,
first, 43 and then "rhyme": 4 3
r m

An appointment for April 16, at four o'clock becomes 4-16-4 and
may be translated "ride ashore": 4 1 6 4
r d sh r

If you learn the system and practice it constantly, you acquire
facility in translation and in interpreting your translations. You
might decide whether you consider the system worth learning
and using by selecting a few numbers that you wish to remember
—such as your social security number, the number of your bank
account, and a telephone number or two—and (1) seeing whether
you can translate them into words or phrases, then (2) deciding
whether you could remember the translations more easily than
the numbers.

As for appointments, it would probably be better to enter your
appointment for April 16 at 4:00 on your calendar than to keep
it on your mind to "ride ashore."

The translation device is useful for the performance of memory
stunts with numbers. But the average person will probably consider it more of a curiosity than a helpful device.

Paired Associates. No one seems to know who originated the
method of paired associates. It appeared in memory systems a long
time ago and has been carefully examined by R. S. Woodworth,
who gives it space in his *Experimental Psychology*.[3]

Read carefully the following pairs of words and try to make an
association between each pair of words:

<pre>
paper . . . . ink
book . . . . cover
essay . . . . poem
wisdom . . . . ignorance
education . . . . . . expense
teacher . . . . pupil
school . . . . building
college . . . . football
university . . . . . . science
</pre>

Now cover the second column and try to supply the second member of each pair from memory. Many people are able to complete most or all of the pairs.

Since associations can be formed so easily, a pair of items can be remembered almost as easily as one item.

The use of key words as the first in each pair of associates is the basis of the Roth Memory Course, an old system which has been promulgated in a number of popular memory-improvement books. The Roth system provided a list of one hundred key words derived from the number-consonant combinations of von Wenaussheim (see page 106). The word for 1 must be a word containing a d or a t and no other consonants in the list, and it must represent a physical object that can be visualized; *hat* meets the requirements. All the one hundred words were chosen in this way. The first ten words of the Roth list are:

1. hat	6. shoe
2. hen	7. cow
3. ham	8. hive
4. hare	9. ape
5. hill	10. woods

The person who wishes to master the Roth system must learn the list of one hundred words so that he knows it as well as he knows the alphabet. Furthermore, he must know each word by number, so that he can instantly give the correct answer if he asks himself, "What is hill?"—5. "What is 8?"—hive.

This list of known words provides the first member of the pair for any number of paired associates. In other words, one may remember a long list of things, in order and out of order, by associating each thing with one of the words in the Roth list.

To illustrate the method, I shall use a very short list of only half a dozen items: (1) book, (2) pen, (3) camera, (4) candy, (5) dress, (6) chair. The trick is to create a picture, the more absurd the better, of the two things in association, such as: (1) a woman wearing a book as a hat, (2) a hen writing with a pen, (3) a man using a ham as a camera, (4) a hare eating candy, (5) an empty dress standing on a hill, (6) a chair with a shoe on one leg. Such absurdities are more easily remembered than more logical associations. Now, what was the fourth item? Well, 4 is hare, and you immediately remember the hare eating candy; so the fourth item was candy. What number was pen? You recall the hen writing with a pen, and hen is 2; so pen was the second item.

It is not a difficult matter for a person with a little imagination and good visual imagery who has thoroughly mastered the key words and has practiced the system for some time to memorize a list of fifty or a hundred objects named by an audience. The audience is, of course, astonished when the performer can correctly say that item number 46 was thermometer.

A series of numbers are remembered by translating the number into a word or phrase and then associating this word or phrase with the proper key word.

A difficulty appears almost immediately with this memory device. If one uses the same list of key words to memorize several lists of things, he will soon experience interference of one list with another. Consequently, it is best to make use of the key words as associates only in material that can be dismissed from the mind after it has been used once or twice.

So the key word system is practically restricted to material that is to be learned for a certain occasion and can soon be forgotten. It is recommended as an indoor sport and for those who see a use for it in their occupation.

Anyone who wishes to give the system a trial on a small scale might learn the first ten key words and practice learning lists of up to ten objects, with friends or members of the family as assistants and audience. Then if he finds the system useful or enjoys the game, he can learn ten more key words which he can originate for himself—and so on. (Key words are formed by the letters-numbers translation system. Thus, 15 would contain t or d, representing 1, and l, representing 5. Vowels do not count, nor do double letters increase the value. So the word for 15 might be a word such as *tile*, *doll*, *till*, *dale*, etc.)

Association Chains. Chaining ideas together by inserting linking associations is a very old device named *catenation* (it was used by the Romans), from the Latin *catena*, chain. In 1848, Hermann Kothe, in Germany, developed a variation of this method which invited ridicule. Unconnected words like *book* and *wagon* may be connected by a bridge of associations as follows: book-read-ride-wagon. The *reductio ad absurdum* of the method is shown by the following illustration: To associate Pat and Mike: Pat-pate-mate-woman-man-Irishman-Mike.

The chain method does not require memorizing an artificial list of key words. The linking words are selected from the thing to be remembered. Below is an illustration of how one could memorize the Gettysburg Address by this method. The linking words are underlined:

Fourscore and seven years ago our fathers brought forth on this continent a new nation, conceived in liberty and dedicated to the proposition that all men are created equal.

Now we are engaged in a great civil war, testing whether that nation, or any nation so conceived and so dedicated, can long endure. We are met on a great battlefield of that war. We have come to dedicate a portion of that field as a final resting place for those who here gave their lives that that nation might live. It is altogether fitting and proper that we should do this.

But, in a larger sense, we cannot dedicate—we cannot consecrate—we cannot hallow this ground. The brave men, living and dead, who struggled here have consecrated it, far above our poor power to add or detract. The world will little note, nor long remember, what we say here, but it can never forget what they did here. It is for us the living, rather to be dedicated here to the unfinished work which they who fought here have thus far so nobly advanced. It is rather for us to be here dedicated to the great task remaining before us—that from these honored dead we take increased devotion to that cause for which they gave the last full measure of devotion; that we here highly resolve that these dead shall not have died in vain—that this nation, under God, shall have a new birth of freedom—and that government of the people, by the people, for the people, shall not perish from the earth.

The underlined words and phrases are then taken from the text and linked together as follows:

Fourscore—battlefield. We associate these words by reflecting that somewhere in the world there is a battlefield laid waste at least once every fourscore years.

Battlefield—brave men, living and dead. We associate by thinking that a battlefield is covered with the bodies of brave men.

Brave men, living and dead—for us. We link these phrases by the thought that the brave men who fought our wars fought for us.

For us—increased devotion. The sacrifices made for us require increased devotion on our part.

Increased devotion—new birth of freedom. These phrases are linked by the thought that increased devotion on our part will bring the country a new birth of freedom.

When we have thoroughly linked these phrases together and have memorized them well, we have blazed a trail through the whole composition. This trail is then used in memorizing the whole address.

The number and selection of ideas to link together requires

judgment, which is developed by experience. Using association chains is easier when you are memorizing a speech of your own, because you are following your own ideas, not those of someone else.

The criticism of chaining is based on the fact that there is less logic in a chain than there is in a well-organized text. You must decide for yourself whether you wish to use this device.

CHAPTER VIII

Some Specific Memory Problems

Now we shall consider some memory problems that need special attention. A number of the principles, techniques, and devices discussed in Chapters V-VII apply to each specific memory problem, and therefore it seems worth while to present here a check list of the topics covered in these chapters.

(A *check list* is a useful supplement to the memory as a way of finding out whether you have forgotten some element of a complicated task. Benjamin Franklin tells in his *Autobiography* how, in his youthful desire to attain moral perfection, he made a list of thirteen virtues he considered essential and how he worked out a system for checking his behavior against this list and for concentrating on each virtue in turn. A student writing a paper would find it useful, before making a final copy, to check his paper against a list of the possible kinds of error in form: (1) spelling, (2) grammar, (3) sentence structure, (4) punctuation, (5) paragraph structure.)

Check List of Memory Principles, Techniques, Devices

General Principles (Chapter V)	Study Methods (Chapter VI)	Memory Devices and Systems (Chapter VII)
1. Interest	1. Environment for study	1. Rhymes
2. Selection		2. Numbering
3. Attention	2. Use of all the senses	3. Alphabetical order
4. Starting right	3. Visual aids	4. Abbreviation
5. Understanding	4. Efficient reading techniques	5. Acrostics
6. Intention to remember	5. Writing as an aid to learning	6. Pigeonholing (spatial arrangement)
7. Confidence		

Check List of Memory Principles, Techniques, Devices (Continued)

General Principles (Chapter V)	Study Methods (Chapter VI)	Memory Devices and Systems (Chapter VII)
8. Ego involvement	6. Recitation (self-testing)	7. Translation (numbers— letters)
9. Meaningful associations	7. Review and use	8. Paired associates
10. Building background	8. Spaced practice	9. Association chains
11. Organization	9. Sleeping over it	
12. Whole and parts	10. Overlearning	
13. Dividing and grouping	11. Finding a principle or pattern	
14. Reinforcement by repetition and use		

As you begin to study each topic in this chapter, glance over this check list to see what items apply to the specific memory problem. As a rule, you will find that most of the principles of Chapter V apply, several of the techniques of Chapter VI apply, and several of the devices discussed in Chapter VII may be used.

Remembering to Do Things. In remembering to do things, first decide whether to do the job mentally or to "remember on paper." What you cannot feel confident of remembering or what can be remembered only by burdening the mind unnecessarily should be put into a written memorandum A chauffeur does not need to rely on a written memorandum to recall how to operate his car, but when going on a long journey he will refer to a road map that tells him what roads to take and where to turn. It would be as impractical to commit to memory a long list of appointments or tasks as it would be for the chauffeur to memorize the road map.

A person who wants to keep his mind clear, well-organized, and working with selective attention to the things that are most important to him can avoid distraction and confusion by making good use of a memorandum on paper. There is no reason for anyone to dispense with desk calendars, appointment books, lists of telephone numbers, shopping lists, and the like if they help him to keep his life organized. There are enough important things that cannot well be put into writing to provide plenty of exercise for the memory.

We might divide our present topic into remembering to do things at a certain *time* and remembering to do things at a certain

place. Two basic principles will guide us one of developing rou-
tines, habits, and skills; the other of careful planning and placing
a paired-associate cue at the right time or place. The second
method calls for an improvement on the old device of tying a
string around the finger, in that the cue is not carried around
on the finger continually, thus losing its potency, but is put,
mentally or physically, at the time when or place where the action
is called for.

(1) *At a certain time.* Some things that you have to do are
matters of routine. It will safeguard you against forgetting them
if you always do routine things in the same order, so that one
task serves as a cue for the next task. Suppose that one of a
housewife's daily chores is to water the plants. Remembering to
water them is easy if she always does it right after washing the
breakfast dishes. Until daily tasks have become habitual, a housewife or a new employee should use a check list of tasks in the
order in which they should be done and do them in that order
until the written list is no longer necessary. A single complicated
task that is repeated frequently should always be done in the same
way: thus, a clerk in a store should always fill out the items of a
sales receipt in the same order.

If you keep a calendar on your desk, you must acquire the
inflexible habit of consulting it the first thing every morning.
If the calendar lists a number of items, your memory task is to
remember the first item, then when it is off your hands, to look
at the calendar for the next item. If you carry a memorandum
pad, you must look at it at regular intervals—for example, just
before going out to lunch if you frequently have chores to do
during your noon hour.

A person who is very busy, who becomes engrossed in his work,
and who may be distracted by unexpected situations needs an
automatic reminder device, like a secretary or an alarm clock.
A woman who wants to remember to call her husband just before
he leaves the office can set the alarm for 4:30 and feel secure that
even if the children are being troublesome or she is watching TV
or snoozing, the alarm will remind her to phone. If she wants to
remember to take a suit to the cleaner, she should lay it out
where she cannot help seeing it frequently. If she wants to
remember to return books to the library while on a shopping trip,
she should put the books with her handbag or in front of the door
by which she will leave to go shopping. If she must remember to

write a letter without delay, she might make a note of it and put the paper in the middle of the floor. To remind yourself to do something which you must do, devise a reminder that cannot fail to remind you.

Sometimes it happens that after going to bed you think of something that you want to or must remember the next day. To be absolutely certain of remembering, get up and make a note of it. But you can be almost as certain of remembering it if you impress it firmly on your mind by repetition and visualize yourself getting up in the morning and remembering it. You must have the firm intention to remember, and confidence. Full confidence will come with the repeated experience of finding that you do remember things the next morning.

(2) *At a certain place.* There is a story which tells how a man who could not remember to do something at a certain place solved the problem by means of an automatic memory device. Every time this man opened his garage door and walked in, a chain hanging inside would swing and hit him. He tried to remember to duck the chain, but when he opened the door he was always in a hurry and preoccupied with other things and would forget the chain. He grew more and more angry with the chain and with himself. Finally, it occurred to him to nail up a small chain on the outside of the door at eye level. This device solved the problem; thereafter he always ducked upon entering the garage.

Remembering to do something at a certain place or in a certain situation is usually possible if you make a strong association between the place, or situation, and the act. If you want to remember to mail a letter on the way to work, you can, of course, hold the letter until you come to the mail box. But suppose you live in a suburb and want to mail the letter in the lobby of the downtown office building where you work. Approaching your office and thinking of what awaits you there, you can easily forget to mail the letter. The thing to do is to visualize yourself entering the building, coming to the spot where the mail box is located, looking at it, thinking of the letter, and putting it in the box. Do this several times with full attention, intention, and confidence. To generalize, project yourself into the future, visualize yourself at the place where you are to do something, and then visualize yourself doing it.

A friend of mine, a professor of marketing, uses this system successfully. When he thinks of a job he must do, he plans when and where he will do it and how he will start. When the time arrives and he finds himself in the place, the associations he has formed between the time and place and the act come to mind. He has found that he can rely on this method, and students to whom he has taught it have found it reliable.

You can use this visualizing device in various ways. If you want to remember to tell So-and-so such-and-such, visualize yourself meeting him and saying what you have to say.

You may, at times, have found yourself worrying lest you have left the door unlocked, left the water or gas or electricity turned on, forgotten to set the alarm, or failed to do some other routine task. Sometimes people start on a trip and either worry themselves sick or return home because of such an uncertainty. When this tendency is extreme, it suggests a general neurotic state of anxiety. But all of us, when overworked or hurried, are apt to have the experience at times. The problem can usually be solved by verbalizing the tasks as we do them (if you can remember to do so). When you wind the clock and set the alarm, say, "I have wound the clock and set the alarm." When you lock the door, say to yourself, "I have locked the door."

After doing this, do not permit yourself to go back to see whether you have set the alarm or have locked the door. It is very easy to develop the habit of checking the door lock two, three, or four times, and such habits are hard to break. Do the task once, "out loud." Say, "Now I have locked the door." Then do not permit yourself to worry about it or check it again.

Remembering Faces and Names. Cornelia Otis Skinner happily confessed in a *Reader's Digest* article that she never remembered a name and always forgot a face. But if we take into consideration that humorists are much given to exaggeration and self-depreciation, we may doubt the literal truth of the lady's confession. At any rate, the ability to recognize faces and remember names is generally regarded as very desirable, and for some people in certain vocations it is a quite necessary ability.

Some people have been conspicuously successful at this memory task. Napoleon and James A. Farley and Charles W. Eliot have been mentioned as having had remarkable memories for people, and it would be easy, if it were worth while, to mention others. But in each case the possessor of such a memory had strong motivation for remembering people and concentrated on this task.

Our problem has three aspects: (1) remembering people, (2) remembering names, and (3) attaching the right name to the right person. Let us consider these in order.

(1) *Remembering people.* The starting point, as with most memory problems, is interest. And the way to build interest, when it is not already there, is with knowledge. If a person learns a great deal about human nature, he is almost sure to become interested in people. The family doctor probably has the advantage of you in his knowledge of people, as he says to himself: "There goes John minus his appendix, but he still has his hernia," or "Mary is digesting her food better since her mother died," or "Here comes Joe, walking as if that ingrown toenail is much improved." If a person could become a physician or a psychiatrist or an anthropologist, his knowledge of people would undoubtedly become such that he would observe people carefully and seldom forget them, even though their names might elude him.

The average person, however, is not going to study people scientifically, even as a hobby. So his problem becomes one of learning more about the people he meets in whatever ways he can. In general, there are two ways of doing this: by asking oneself some fundamental question about the character of everyone one meets, and by gathering information about people.

One's powers of observation are improved if he searches for the answer to a question. So in observing people you may well pose to yourself some broad question about them which will require careful observation to answer. For instance, is Harry always laughing and joking because he is happy or because he is trying to escape from or hide unhappiness? To answer this question, you must study Harry carefully over a period of some time. Posing some such question with each person you meet will surely improve your understanding of people and your interest in them.

The second way to increase one's knowledge of people and one's interest in them is simply to gather facts about them systematically. You might keep a notebook in which to record facts and observations about everyone you meet. Get in the habit of noting physical characteristics, mental characteristics, emotional characteristics, and of comparing people in these respects.

In order to become a skilled observer of people, one must be able to classify their physical and mental traits, as a scientist classifies phenomena. One cannot learn to distinguish one plant

from another until he learns to observe that this plant has opposite leaves and that one alternate leaves, this one has a smooth
stem and that one a hairy stem, this one has a flower with five
petals and that one a flower with six petals, and so on. Applying
the principle to people, you can, for example, classify faces by
shape, as round, oval, square, long, broad, heart-shaped, pear-
shaped.

(2) *Remembering names.* Our second problem is that of remembering names, and the same basic principles will guide us
again. To remember names, you must gather information about
them and so become interested in them. A good way to do this
is to learn something about their historical development and
national characteristics.

As people multiplied and began to crowd together, surnames
developed to provide better individual identification. The Hebrew
system was to identify a person by his parents, as Joshua, the
Son of Nun; Caleb, the Son of Jephunneh. Later on, when personal names became too common, place of residence was added
as a more complete identifying mark: Judas of Galilee, Simon of
Cyrene. Sometimes a person was known in more than one way,
as Simon the Canaanite, or Simon the Zealot.

The Romans had a more precise nomenclature than most other
peoples. The Roman freeman had three names. The first, the
praenomen, was the personal, or "given" name; the second, the
nomen, was a clan, or tribal, name; the third, the *cognomen,*
corresponded to our surname. So we find names such as Marcus
Tullius Cicero and Quintus Horatius Flaccus.

The old Germans took names from such qualities as greatness,
sublimity, beauty, bravery, and wealth; for instance, Walter,
meaning *mighty;* Ewald, or Adelwald, meaning *noble;* Willigis,
meaning *very strong;* Irfried, meaning *defense of honor.*

In England the crowding and traveling that called for more
definite names followed the Norman Conquest. In all parts of
Europe surnames were adopted at about the same time. People
holding property added the names of their holdings or castles
to their given names, leading to the custom of designating the
whole family by the same name. The country folk followed by
using place names such as Hill, Dale, Wood, etc. And surnames
such as "the Son of Richard, Robert, or John" became Richard-
son, Robertson, Johnson.

In modern German names, when two words go to make up a person's last name, it is safe to assume that the person is Jewish. Jews, not being citizens at the time that Germany and Austria required the use of surnames, had to add a word to their original names to distinguish them from the citizens. Hence such names as Applebaum (apple tree), Steinhaus (stone house).

The Irish took surnames from the following sources: personal names, rank or occupation, the animal, vegetable, or mineral kingdoms, localities, and personal peculiarities or attributes. The letter O (for of) before a name, as in O'Hara, reliably indicates an Irish name.

A name beginning with Mac- or Mc- may be either Irish or Scottish. These prefixes mean "son of."

The Dutch and Scandinavians often changed their names into surnames by the addition of -sen. If a Dutchman were baptized Henrick Jansen, his son, if baptized Tunis, would be called Tunis Henricksen, and the son of the latter, if called William, would have the name William Tunissen.

Once surnames were adopted and became reasonably permanent, the abrasive effect of time produced numerous varieties of the same name: Ralph, Rolf; Rowes, Rowson; Rawlins, Rawlinson.

The same names, too, slipped into various languages, with changes such as: (French) Karre—(English) Gary—(German) Gehring.

Russian names often end in a v or a y. Italian names usually end in a vowel. All information of this kind that builds up a body of knowledge about names makes them more interesting and memorable.

There are, of course, more immediate ways of relating names and making them distinctive. One of these is classification. Everyone classifies to some extent alphabetically. A name beginning with a less common letter, such as Q, Y, or Z is distinctive. Or names may be classified by length, and long or extremely short names are distinctive. In trying to remember a name, you not only pay special attention to the letter with which it begins, its length, number of syllables, and rhythm, but you pay attention to such things as—does it have double letters? is the same letter repeated at intervals? does it end with the same letter with which it begins? does it contain i's or t's to be dotted or crossed? does it have letters like h or l that extend above the others, or letters like g or y that extend below the line? Every name is distinctive in several such ways.

The most interesting and distinctive names are those that have an obvious meaning. There are the Whites, Blacks, Littles, Walkers, Hoppers, Drinkwaters, Armstrongs.

(3) *Attaching the right name to the right person.* The problem of fitting the name to the person is not easy, because the face is something seen and the name is something heard. Associating them is somewhat like associating colors and sounds.

In associating a face and a name, it is important to be careful of the direction in which one makes the association. If you expect to meet a person and to recall his name upon seeing him, you should make the association from his physical appearance to his name. If you expect to come upon the name and recall the appearance of the person upon seeing the name, make the association from the name to the physical appearance.

As one usually has to form his associations quickly, while being introduced, it is very important to form habits, and good ones, of attaching name to person. The two most important of these habits are those of finding distinctiveness and meaning in the face-name combination, and the habit of application. Let us examine these in turn.

Sometimes the name does, in some way, suggest the man. Of all the Whites, some are light-haired and fair-complexioned. Some of the Blacks or Schwartzes are dark people. Some Shorts are short, some Littles and Kleins are little, some Baers are big and hairy. Some names of foreign origin are attached to people who have facial characteristics that we consider typical of that nationality.

Then it sometimes happens that a person has physical characteristics which, by using your imagination and exaggerating certain features as a cartoonist might, you can associate with the name. Thus, knowing that a Mr. Zimmerman is of German ancestry, you can try to see him as a German although he does not have obviously Teutonic features. A tall, handsome, or distinguished-looking man named King you can endow with regal qualities. If Mr. Berg (mountain) is of more than ordinary size, you can look at him as a man-mountain. You can magnify the virtues of a Mr. Goodman, or Gutman; and if he looks the part at all, you can make a hero out of Mr. Knight. If a Mr. Fisher or a Mr.

Hunter is a salesman, you can easily think of him as fishing or hunting for sales. (But it would not be useful to picture Mr. Hunter on a horse or carrying a gun if you will be meeting him in an office.)

Still staying within the realm of meaningful associations, you can make use of a contradiction between the person and his name. A small Mr. King could be the Little King. A swarthy Mr. Day could be remembered as a dark Day. Of a large Mr. Klein, you could tell yourself that Mr. Klein is not at all *klein*. A fat Mr. Byrd you could remember as too fat a Byrd to fly. Mr. Fox is not at all foxy. Mr. Altman is not an old man yet. Mr. Gold is not rich.

A common name like Jones or Johnson may remind you of someone else you have known by that name; then you might think, this is the red-haired Jones, or the dentist Jones, or Wellington Jones.

The more associations you can make with a thing, the better it is remembered. Often, when introducing a stranger to us, a person will identify or describe him in some way, such as "Mary used to work with me at Snordley's" or "Mr. Pendleton is our Personnel Director." So whatever you learn about a person should be fitted into a complex of facts, feelings, and memories about the person, including, of course, such things as his occupation, family, hobbies, ideas, and life history.

The second habit to be formed is that of application and use. It is sometimes easy to remember a face and a name separately but difficult to connect them at that important moment when the person appears. One should reinforce the memory of the name by use and strengthen the association between the person and his name by using the name in speaking to the person. Do so at the earliest opportunity by repeating his name when you meet him: "I'm glad to meet you, Mr. Jones." If you are not whisked away to meet other people but remain to talk with Mr. Jones, use his name now and then (not too often), and use it in saying good-bye.

You must, of course, be sure you got the name right! If you did not hear it well or if there is some doubt about how it is spelled, ask to have the name repeated or spelled. You should not be embarrassed to do so. Mr. X will be flattered that you are sufficiently interested in his name to want to get it right.

You sometimes want to remember the whole name of a person —if you have just established a first-name relationship with him or if you might want to address a letter to him. Then learn the whole name as a unit: Fred Z. Jones, not just Jones.

If you meet many people in your business or professional or social life, you have to do some practicing to remember those recently met. You will probably keep a notebook in which you list everyone you expect and want to meet again. You should review the names in this book now and then. And you can do some practicing before you have a chance to write down the names of new acquaintances. At a party or meeting, when you are not talking you can glance about now and then and review the names and restudy the faces of people you have met shortly before.

Most people, in entering the names of new acquaintances in a notebook, merely put down the name and address and perhaps the phone number. But some people have to make a fuller record —for example, a physician, a lawyer, a salesman. According to your needs and purposes, you can jot down a description of the person and some facts about him, or just put down his full name and address.

Remembering faces and names is not a gift; it is a skill, comparable with playing tennis. Anyone can acquire the skill if he is willing to learn and practice the game.

Remembering Numbers.   The recall of numbers presents the problem that all numbers are abstract symbols with little or no inherent meaning or interest. The meanings of numbers are to be found in the things with which they are associated and in their combinations.

People with good memories for numbers usually learn a great many "higher units" which they recognize within the miscellaneous numbers presented to them. It is these recognized higher units that enable them to organize and remember the new combinations.

Let us try a few illustrative higher units. The number 5 is easy to remember. Then, 25 is just as easy to remember as 5, if you know that 25 is the square of 5; 625 is easy to remember, if you recall that it is 25 squared; and 390,625 is easy to remember, if you know that it is the square of 625.

A number can derive meaning in many ways. The number 36, for instance, has meaning as the square of 6; as an "even" number; and as being divisible by either 4 or 9. It would have other meanings for you if you had just lost 36 dollars, or if you were 36 years old, or if you had 36 grandchildren, or if there were just 36 days from today to the date of your next vacation.

You can improve your memory for numbers through constant application of the foregoing suggestions: in brief, master numerous higher units and then find associated meanings for these higher units.

A good illustration of the way one's memory for numbers may be improved is to be found in the experience of Salo Finkelstein. This man was a clerk in a small office in Lodz, Poland, when a "lightning calculator" came to town and astonished the public with his performances. Finkelstein tried to imitate the entertainer and found out, as he says, that memory is the most important aspect of mental calculation. So he began to develop his own memory for numbers and gradually discovered that he could be successful both in recall and in calculation. He started to give demonstrations of his own. Finally, he traveled throughout Europe and eventually came to the United States to display his ability. In the Presidential election of 1932, he demonstrated his skill by adding the votes as they were announced and giving the radio audience minute-by-minute statements of the comparative standing of the various candidates.

Having some scientific curiosity about his own abilities, Finkelstein came to New York University and allowed us to study his unusual memory for numbers. His ability was extraordinary, even though he told us that when he began practicing (he was then a clerk in Poland), it was little better than average. Now he was able to perform remarkable feats of memory; for example, he could memorize a series of thirty digits in three seconds. He explained his method of memorizing a long number such as 1415926535897-93238462643383279. He simply broke the number up, mentally, into small numbers, each of which had some meaning or association for him:

141: the square root of 2.

592: with 10 in front (10592) it is the telephone number of the P & F manufacturing plant in Lodz; also 2595 is the number of paragraphs in Spinoza's *Ethics*; further, 2,592,000 is the number of seconds in a month.

6535 and 8979: the 5's and 9's are repeated; 89 and 79 are both prime numbers.

3238: seen as 32 and 38; the tens figure is repeated

462: composed of even numbers.

643: with 1 in front (1643) is the birth date of Newton and the year the barometer was invented.

383: a nice symmetrical number.

279: 2 plus 7 is 9.

It is clear that Finkelstein's feats of memory were possible because of a tremendous amount of prior memorizing.

Note that in memorizing this long number, Finkelstein utilized the two most effective methods: he made use of higher units when he thought of 141 as the square root of 2; and he found an associated meaning when he identified 1643 as the birth date of Newton.

Let us analyze the two methods again, as exemplified in Finkelstein's work. Below are some higher units that he used without a moment's hesitation, showing that he knew them as well as we know the name Mississippi. Here is the way he explains how he developed these higher units:

"Today I found out that 181 is a prime number. I will associate it that way from now on and remember it without thought. One time I had to calculate mentally the square of 729, which is 531,441, and the cube of 729, which is 387,420,489, and this squared, which is 150,094,635,296,999,121; 999 is 37 x 27 and 121 is the square of 11. I have always remembered these combinations since."

One day when asked what associations he had with 5584, a number picked at random, he hesitated a moment and then said, "37 squared is 1369, a permutation of 1396, which multiplied by four gives 5584; 349 multiplied by 2 raised to the fourth power also gives 5584; 348 is also the greatest prime number in 5584."

It is unnecessary to continue these illustrations. Finkelstein could provide them by the hour, for he seldom let a day go by without learning some association for a group of numbers.

It is possible for those who have only a limited knowledge of mathematics to see a pattern in many numbers. The pattern is obvious in 1234, 6789, 5432, 1357, 4680, 9753, 9764, 1298, 3377, 3337, 3777, 3737, 3773, 1324, 12305, 364656—is it not? You can, if you try, see a pattern in figures when it is not immediately apparent. For example:

1359: series of odd numbers, but 9 replaces 7.

1537: similar, but you skip 3 and then come back to it.

2467: series of even numbers, but you get tired at the end and add 1 instead of 2.
6242: all even numbers; 62 is larger than 42.
2439: 2, square of 2, 3, square of 3.
13610: $1 + 2 = 3$, $3 + 3 = 6$, $6 + 4 = 10$.
1236: $1 + 2 + 3 = 6$.
3721: $3 \times 7 = 21$.

Most of us do not have the ability, the time, nor the desire to become professionals like Finkelstein, but if we apply his methods as best we can, we shall doubtless achieve notable improvement in our memory for numbers.

With some numbers—those representing quantities, values, and dates—it is desirable to have an idea of the approximate quantity, value, or time. Thus, to avoid thinking of 93,000 or 93,000,000,000 miles as the average distance from the earth to the sun, you must have a good idea of distances in our solar system. A thoughtless child may work arithmetic problems and be satisfied with ridiculous answers: e.g., the average weight of the four men is 15.6 pounds. It would be an absent-minded or careless student in college who would give the date of Milton's birth as 1806 (for 1608). So: place your precise number within the area of the possible or the reasonable.

It is often sufficient to remember only "round" numbers. For anyone but an astronomer, 93,000,000 is close enough for the average distance in miles from the earth to the sun. A Frenchman once figured and memorized π (pi, ratio of circumference to diameter of a circle) to seven hundred decimals, but for ordinary purposes it is sufficient to remember 3.1416-. For all but scholars it suffices to remember that Chaucer was born in the fourteenth century and died in the fifteenth. The more important the number and the nearer it is to other associated numbers that are approximately equal to it in size, the more necessary it is to learn the precise number. Thus, it is quite all right, for general purposes, to place King Alfred in the ninth century, but it is not satisfactory to place Abraham Lincoln in the nineteenth century and let it go at that. It is not enough to place the attack on Pearl Harbor in 1941; if you are going to remember the date, you must remember the whole date: December 7, 1941.

One final precaution: in working with numbers, be very careful to get them right, and avoid learning mistakes that can be costly.

If you write down a number, for instance, make your figures care-fully so that you will not take a 7 for a 1, a 9 for a 4, and so on.

A memory for numbers is not very hard to develop, provided only that we are willing to work with numbers and make them our own.

Spelling. In regard to spelling, English is the most lawless of languages. The sound of an English word is not always a key to its spelling; *word* could be spelled *weard, werd, wird,* or *wurd* without violating any rules of English orthography. Still there are some rules of spelling and some phonetic principles (*physophy* is not a possible spelling of *philosophy,* nor *convient* of *convenient*).

There are intelligent, even brilliant, people whose spelling is atrocious, and there are many students who succeed in graduating from college but who spell badly. One can only infer that people who demonstrate superior mental ability but who cannot spell have never been sufficiently interested in spelling to master it. One can easily understand that there are people who are much interested in facts and ideas but see no significance in spelling—nothing but a set of conventionalities. For a logical person, it is annoying that the sound *wensday* is spelled *Wednesday* because in Old English it was *Wodnes daeg,* the day devoted to the god Woden. Spelling is, to a certain extent, merely a matter of eti-quette, of conforming to custom.

Children who do not master the general principles of spelling establish habits of spelling many words incorrectly and as adults lack the ambition and courage to make a new start. Having written *Wensday* hundreds of times, it never occurs to them to think of spelling it otherwise. If one does discover that he has been misspelling a word and wants to establish the habit of spelling it correctly, the technique of negative practice is the best way of breaking the bad habit and forming a new one (see page 54).

One reason for poor spelling is that when people are writing they are thinking—as they should be—of what they are saying and are not thinking of spelling. If they have the habit of spelling correctly, good. But what about the person whose spelling habits are poor? His only recourse, if he cares whether his spelling is good or bad, is to write without thinking of spelling and then proofread what he has written, thinking only of spelling. Of course, many people have difficulty seeing spelling errors, espe cially their own, but careful proofreading will result in the correction of some obvious errors.

Motivation for improving one's spelling might come from the realization that many people consider poor spelling an indication of poor intelligence or poor education, and they note the one word in a hundred that is misspelled without giving the writer credit for spelling ninety-nine words correctly. (You may be wearing a beautiful new shirt, but if there is a little spot on the collar, people see the spot rather than the rest of the shirt.)

Most of the words misspelled in college students' papers are the common words. If a student uses a word like *hieroglyphic*, he will take thought about it and, if he is doubtful, look it up in a dictionary. But he may use *to* for *too* or *there* for *their*. The reason is that he is not thinking of spelling when writing these words. Most spelling errors are due to carelessness. To repeat, the only remedy for careless misspelling is to become spelling-conscious and to establish the proofreading habit. (Many students are too indifferent, too much in a hurry, to proofread their writings.)

It is an inefficient use of time and energy to check on individual words or forms of words without learning the rules of phonetics or the few rules of spelling, such as those about *ie* and *ei* and when to double a consonant. Typical errors of college students which are due to failure to learn the rules are: *recieve, beleive, comeing, noticable, begining, dinning room, occurence, tryed*. Failure to consider the laws of phonetics results in such errors as *physcology* (for *psychology*), *convience* (for *convenience*), and *peacable*.

Some spelling errors are due to incorrect pronunciation, as in *atheletic* or *incidently*.

One important fact to take into consideration in connection with English spelling is that to understand the meaning and remember the spelling of words derived from Latin and Greek— mostly abstract, scholarly, scientific, and technical words—it is necessary to have some knowledge of Latin and Greek stems and prefixes. How can you learn and remember the meaning of a term like *azoic* unless you know that *a-* is a prefix meaning *not* and *-zo-* means *life*?

An adult who has completed his schooling is probably not going to study Latin and Greek to improve his knowledge of

English words and spelling. But he can acquire an interest in derivation. Whenever he looks up a word in the dictionary, he can note the derivation and thus build up a knowledge of common stems and prefixes. (A certain amount of such knowledge is acquired without effort. Everyone knows that an *atheist* is a person who does *not* believe in God; without thinking about it, he interprets the *a-* as *not*, and he knows that *-the-* in this word means God because he knows other words like *theology* and *theism*.)

One who wishes to make a general attack on his poor spelling habits should buy and study a popular book for adults on the improvement of spelling or on vocabulary building. Such books present the common Latin and Greek stems and prefixes in a systematic way. And the spelling book will give and explain the rules of spelling, which are not at all difficult to learn if one is interested in learning them.

The spelling of some difficult words cannot be determined by the spelling rules, the principles of phonetics, or a knowledge of derivation. Such words have to be memorized, just as new words do in the study of a foreign language.

You should look for patterns in difficult words. The spelling of *Mississippi* is easy once you have noticed the pattern: after *M* comes *i-ss-i-ss-i-pp-i*, double consonants sandwiched between *i*'s. You can remember the pairs of double consonants in *embarrass*, *accommodate*, *occurrence*.

In learning the spelling of a difficult word, it is necessary to concentrate on the difficult letter or letters—the whole word will not be difficult. Thus, difficulty is caused by the first *a* in *separate*, the final *e* in *envelope*, the lack of final *e* in *develop*, the second *s* in *ecstasy*, the *l*'s in *parallel*, the *i* and *e* which may be transposed in *sacrilegious*.

Confusing similar words must have special attention: *to* and *too*; *there*, *their*, and *they're*; *allusion* and *illusion*. Books on spelling contain lists of such words, as well as lists of difficult words.

Perhaps the chief difficulty for poor spellers is that no one corrects them. Competent teachers of English correct their students' spelling errors, but many teachers of history, science, and other subjects fail to do so. People you write to do not return your letters with the spelling errors marked. A businessman who has a stenographer leaves spelling to the stenographer, and an author relies on the publisher's editor to correct his spelling. It is difficult to learn anything if your errors are not corrected. If you are to improve your spelling you must become your own teacher, relying on the authority of books.

Foreign Languages. An American usually considers learning a foreign language a very difficult task, and perhaps an unnatural or unnecessary task. Europeans do not feel that way about languages because they are only a few dozen or a few hundred miles from countries where other languages are spoken. In Switzerland, where it is hardly more than a stone's throw to a foreign country, most of the residents speak the languages of their near neighbors: the Germans, the French, and the Italians.

A psychologist friend of mine, a native of Hungary, had to learn Latin, Greek, French, and German to be considered a well-educated person. Then, in order to find out what was being done in psychology in England and the United States, he learned English. Europeans do not consider learning a new language a very arduous task. The linguist finds resemblances in the words and grammar of different languages and so learns easily and remembers well.

In learning a foreign language, interest and enthusiasm are of the greatest importance. It is necessary to be interested in the country, or countries, whose language you are studying.

Interest is further heightened if you can find someone whose native language is the one you are studying to converse with, and if you can obtain newspapers and magazines in that language.

You can benefit from use of foreign newspapers and magazines even while your knowledge of the language is meager. Pictures and advertisements have short and simple captions which can often be translated with the help of the illustrations. When you have a fair knowledge of vocabulary and grammar, you can read articles on current events and find them easy to understand because you may have read of the same events in English.

Subscribing to a foreign newspaper or magazine also provides the benefit of good spaced practice, since it comes at regular intervals.

In learning the vocabulary of a foreign language, it is wise to use the card system. Some words closely resembling English words you will learn at once without much effort. Other words may need a good deal of practice before they are firmly fixed in your mind. In writing the words on cards, write the foreign word on one side and the English word on the other. Always try to translate the word before looking at the other side of the card. (You do not really know the word until you can think of it easily when you look at the English equivalent.) When you feel that you know a word well, take it out of the pack and substitute a new word that needs practice. Carry a pack of such words with you and use scattered moments of time, as when you are traveling on a bus or subway or waiting for dinner, to practice your vocabulary.

The factor of attention is extremely important. You must start right by pronouncing each new word correctly and noting its spelling, its gender (if it is a noun), its conjugation (if it is a verb), and its irregularities, if any.

If the foreign word resembles its English equivalent, note the differences in pronunciation and spelling. Thus, in learning the German word *national*, be sure to pronounce it *natzionál*. Note suggestions of related English words: associate the Spanish *sol* sun, with our word *solar*. Break up misleading associations: Spanish *ropa* means *clothes*, not *rope*; *desgraciado* means *unfortunate*, not *disgraced*.

If there is no resemblance between the foreign word and its English equivalent, you can only tie the two together by repeating them a number of times, say ten times on the first learning: "*l'eau*, the water, *l'eau*, the water," and so on. Later you will reinforce this learning by review and use.

Each time you repeat a foreign word, think of both the sound and the appearance of the *word* and also of the *thing*—object, action, or relationship—symbolized by the word. For *eau*, think of water, water to drink, water in rivers and oceans, water, water everywhere. This procedure is necessary if you are to learn to think in the foreign language.

Tie related foreign words together, as German *national* with *die Nation* and *die Nationalität*.

It is absolutely necessary to tie idioms as well as words together. Though many foreign words and English words are as interchangeable as an American cent and a Guatemalan centavo, there are many that change their value according to their use. In French and Spanish, different words for *time* are used according to whether you are speaking of a period of time or of the time of day, and you do not say "How old is he?" but "What age does he have?" In German you do not "close the door"; you "make the door to." The problem that needs most attention after you have learned a small basic vocabulary is this problem of idioms and of using the right word in the right situation.

For the student of a foreign language a great deal of reciting, or self-testing, in the form of writing is necessary. This is especially true in learning declensions and conjugations.

A good teacher will stress all these things, and so will a good textbook if you do not have a teacher.

Memorizing Literature, Speeches, Etc. In this section we consider the memorizing, or "learning by heart," of published poetry or prose and also the learning of lectures, speeches, and stories, which may or may not be learned verbatim.

We may assume that in everything of this sort there will be a theme and the material will be organized around this theme. The first step toward memorizing this kind of material is to identify the theme and understand it clearly.

We may divide the material to be learned into those things which must be learned verbatim and those that can be presented in the language of the moment. College lectures and many speeches are of the kind in which the precise language can be varied from one occasion to the next. In these cases, all that one needs to remember are the theme and the basic organization. Here the specific language used is of little importance, provided that it is clear and adequate.

In learning a formal speech or sermon, the outline is the part that should be studied most thoroughly until its themes and logic become crystal clear. Many speakers need help in memorizing such material. Mark Twain, we will remember, drew pictures for this purpose. Some speakers write their outlines separately; others underline key sentences in their written speeches. Some use abbreviations, which they associate and remember.

Few speakers use the very same words each time they make a speech unless they merely read it to the audience. But most speakers like to memorize some parts of a speech. They may feel that certain memorized phrases are particularly eloquent or provide just the emphasis they want; furthermore, they may wish to use quotations that must be repeated accurately. Here, again, excerpts must be given close attention and fitted properly into the whole speech.

In telling humorous stories, we must find a general theme with a "punch line" that has to be delivered precisely to insure the desired effect. A most common failure in storytelling consists of remembering and stating the theme but misplacing the "punch line."

In verbatim learning of prose and poetry, an important factor is familiarity with the author's language and concepts and with the rhythm of his writing. A psychologist once remarked that he had memorized Edmund Spenser's *Faerie Queene* (written in old English) as an experiment and that he found himself learning more than ten times as fast at the end as he had at the beginning —because he had learned Spenser's language and ideas. Actors often have this kind of experience; it is said that a second play of Shakespeare's is much easier to memorize than the first.

In learning long pieces, spacing and review are, of course, of utmost importance, but we have discussed these adequately. The whole versus the part method, however, needs further consideration.

The whole and part problem has two aspects; one has to do with mere quantity, the other with organization. The longer a piece is, the harder it is to grasp it as a unit. The poorer the organization, or the less well it is understood, the more apt we are to forget its parts. I can illustrate these two factors from my own experience. When I was in grammar school I learned Lewis Carroll's "The Walrus and the Carpenter," verse by verse— because it seemed to me then too long to read and reread from beginning to end. While writing this section dealing with the whole and part methods, I decided to test myself by reciting this poem. I started with considerable confidence:

> The sea was wet as wet could be,
>   The sands were dry as dry.
> You could not see a cloud, because
>   No cloud was in the sky:
> No birds were flying overhead—
>   There were no birds to fly.
>
> The Walrus and the Carpenter
>   Were walking close at hand;
> They wept like anything to see
>   Such quantities of sand:
> "If this were only cleared away,"
>   They said, "it would be grand."

At this point I stopped and could remember no more. When I looked up the poem, I was surprised to find that I had not started at the first, but at the third, verse. The two verses I recited were given correctly, but I had been able to remember only two verse-units of the poem. This was the result of learning by the part method.

Experimental studies to determine the values of the whole and part methods began in 1900, when experimental laboratories were still a novelty. Lottie Steffens, at that time, began to wonder what would be the best way to learn a poem. She had a number of adults learn a nine-line stanza and observed that they read and reread separate parts and worked in no very systematic manner. Would it be easier or harder, she wondered, to master the whole poem at once by reading it from beginning to end each time? With five adults and two children as subjects, she carried on a series of experiments in learning verses and nonsense syllables. In this study the whole method came out better every time, and for both kinds of subject matter. The least advantage obtained was two per cent and the greatest was twenty-six per cent. The average was twelve per cent in favor of the whole method.[1]

The Steffens experiment was the forerunner of a whole series of experiments on the same problem, all of which pointed in the same general direction. The whole method has been reported as best under certain circumstances and with certain limitations.

It has been found that nearly everyone has a certain resistance to using the whole method. This resistance must be overcome by practice and training in order to achieve the best results. The success of the method often surprises the persevering learner.

The advantage of the whole method is that as learning goes on, the poem, prose piece, or similar composition is organized as it should be. Where associations are made, they remain. Everything is always in place, and whatever is memorized lasts longer than it does with the part method.

But the part method has some value, too. Results begin to show up very soon, and this is motivating. "Something accomplished, something done" makes one feel better about his memorizing. The part method does not require any unnecessary overlearning of easy parts in order that certain harder parts can be remembered.

A person cannot always learn a whole poem as a unit. He will usually find it advisable, however, to memorize in as large units as he can master, and, finally, to combine these units. The intelligence and maturity of the learner as well as his familiarity with the kind of subject matter he is learning are factors of importance in deciding the size of the units learned. The more intelligent the learner, the more he will be able to grasp the meaning of the whole unit and, in consequence, the better he will memorize by the whole method. Children, with more limited grasp, will not be so successful in attempting to grasp the whole meaning at once, just as they will be in more need of the encouragement that comes from the mastery of the shorter and easier parts. Familiarity with the material also makes it possible to grasp longer units.

The nature of the subject matter, too, will have considerable bearing on the method used. A person learning a speech will usually do well to learn it by the whole method. The continuity of a speech is often very important; if the speaker forgets a portion in the middle, he may not be able to make use of the remaining sections.

Carl I. Hovland summarizes the two methods as follows: The learner, he says, gets the feeling of success more quickly with the part method. The parts become subgoals that lead toward the main goal, and the satisfaction in reaching the subgoals is very helpful. The whole method requires so much more time and effort before results are visible that it is discouraging. The experienced learner, however, understands that, although the results are delayed, the whole method will prove itself more efficient in the long run.[2]

Woodworth summarizes the matter by saying that the best approach is to start with the whole method and then compromise by concentrating on parts to the extent that this is necessary.[3]

Even when you learn by using the whole method, at some places the links will be weak—at ends of paragraphs, at ends of verses, and perhaps at other points where the transition is rather abrupt. *Strengthen the weak links.*

CHAPTER IX

Conclusion

Since memory results from learning, and learning is a skill, improvement in learning and, therefore, in remembering can be achieved. As learning becomes more significant and more rapid, the stored wealth of memory, based on such learning, can be more wisely invested in selected interests. The memory can be trained to function more efficiently and, in certain cases, the extent of improvement can be very great. Some people possess more aptitude and can progress more rapidly than others. But anyone who gives careful thought to his methods of learning can improve his memory.

As memory is part of the mechanism of adjusting to life, it can be expected that particular memories will be frequently changed by the redefinitions that come with a person's wider experience and with the new patterns that develop from his new goals and new information. The memory is a dynamic organization of ideas by which the individual interprets his environment and lives. It is not, as some have thought, merely a quantity, a bucketful, of inert thoughts left over from the past.

It is true that those who live most remember most. This statement does not refer to people who are always in such a hurry that their time of life is crowded with trivia. It does not refer to those who are so confused by minutiae of everyday living that nothing has real significance for them. The *law of effect* provides the basic explanation of our statement. Memory is the *reward* of meaningful experience.

People who remember most possess the attitude of an explorer, for they do explore particular things of their own choosing. They have interests and follow them. They want to know more and more and more; their memory "ownership" is very personal. They identify themselves with their learning experiences so closely that every memory mirrors a different aspect of their own careers. The accumulation of memories enriches their egos, whereas the ideas which they find repugnant are buried in their unconscious minds and forgotten. Fortunate is the person with a memory that can accept, absorb, and cling to rewarding experiences and with little need to bury embarrassing parts of the self in his subconscious.

But memory is not simply an emotional experience which caters to the individual's pleasure; it is also a matter of reasoning. Thinking and remembering function together as acts of the same brain and nervous system. It is difficult to recall what has not been understood, and it is hard to forget what has been thoroughly and carefully thought through. Principles that string ideas together like beads bind them as with chains. Orderly material put away in an orderly mind seldom gets lost. Thoughts that are well organized are also well remembered.

Since learning and remembering are activities, they are embodied in techniques—such techniques, for instance, as care in starting right, in spacing continuing efforts, in naming, in remembering locations, in associating in the right direction, in classifying. This book has described many of these techniques, and there is no need to repeat what has been said. The use of the methods described will promote the achievement of a good memory.

Good fortune, reader, and may happy memories attend you.

REFERENCES

Chapter I:

(1) Tredgold, A. F. "Idiots Savants," in *An Outline of Abnormal Psychology*. Ed., Gardner Murphy. New York: The Modern Library, 1929. P. 25.
(2) Woodworth, Robert S. *Experimental Psychology*. New York: Henry Holt and Company, 1938. P. 193.
(3) Woodworth, Robert S. *Psychology*. 3rd ed. New York: Henry Holt and Company, 1934. P. 294.
(4) Munn, Norman L. *The Fundamentals of Human Psychology*. Boston: Houghton Mifflin Company, 1956. P. 279.
(5) James, William. *Principles of Psychology*. New York: Henry Holt and Company, 1890. Reprinted, 1950. Vol. I, p. 667.
(6) Hovland, Carl I. "Human Learning and Retention," in *Handbook of Experimental Psychology*. Ed., S. S. Stevens. New York: John Wiley & Sons, Inc., 1951. P. 661.

Chapter III:

(1) Plato, "Phaedo," in *The Dialogues of Plato*. Tr., Benjamin Jowett. New York: Horace Liveright, 1927. Pp. 68, 71.
(2) James, William. *Psychology—Briefer Course*. New York: Henry Holt and Company, 1892. P. 294.
(3) Penfield, Wilder. "Brain's Record of Past a Continuous Movie Film," *Science News Letter* (April 27, 1957), 265.
(4) Morrow, Robert S., and Cohen, Jacob. "The Diagnostic Memory Scale: I, Comparison of Brain Damaged Patients and Normal Controls," *Transactions of the New York Academy of Science*, XIV (1952), 241-246.
(5) Lindsley, Donald B. In *Fields of Psychology*. Ed., R. S. Seashore. New York: Henry Holt and Company, 1947. P. 145.
(6) Morgan, Clifford T. "Localization of Memory Functions in the Brain," in *Handbook of Experimental Psychology*. New York: J. Wiley & Sons, Inc., 1951. P. 780.
(7) *Ibid.* P. 784.
(8) Guilford, J. P. *Laboratory Studies in Psychology*. New York: Henry Holt and Company, 1934. P. 122.

(9) Allport, W. G., and Postman, Leo. *The Psychology of Rumor.* New York: Henry Holt and Company, 1947. P. 111.

(10) Bartlett, F. C. *Remembering.* Cambridge University Press, 1932. Pp. 169-171.

Chapter IV:

(1) Burtt, H. E. "An Experimental Study of Early Childhood Memory," *Journal of Genetic Psychology,* XL (1932), 287-295.

(2) James, William. *Principles of Psychology.* New York: Henry Holt and Company, 1890. Reprinted, 1950. Vol. I, p. 681, fn.

(3) Prince, Morton. *The Unconscious.* New York: The Macmillan Company, 1914. P. 401.

(4) Thompson, Clara, and Mullahy, Patrick. *Psychoanalysis: Evolution and Development.* New York: Hermitage House, 1950. Pp. 93-94.

(5) "Memories Before Birth," *Time,* June 8, 1953.

(6) Asher, E. J., Tiffin, J., and Knight, F. B. *Introduction to General Psychology.* New York: D. C. Heath and Company, 1953. P. 209.

(7) Woodworth, Robert S., and Marquis, D. G. *Psychology.* 5th ed. New York: Henry Holt and Company, 1947. P. 556.

(8) Weitzenhoffer, Andre M. *Hypnotism.* New York: John Wiley & Sons., Inc., 1953. Pp. 165-177.

(9) Hunt, J. McV. *Personality and Behavior Disorders.* New York: Ronald Press Company, 1944. P. 1007.

(10) Morrow, R. S., and Cohen, Jacob. "The Diagnostic Memory Scale: I, Comparison of Brain Damaged Patients and Normal Controls," *Transactions of the New York Academy of Science,* XIV (1952), 241-246.

(11) Halstead, W. C. "Preliminary Analysis of Grouping Behavior in Patients with Cerebral Injury by the Method of Equivalent and Nonequivalent Stimuli," *American Journal of Psychiatry,* XCVI (1940), 1263-1294.

(12) Menninger, Karl A. *The Human Mind.* 3rd ed. New York: Alfred A. Knopf, 1949. P. 185.

(13) Störring, Gustav. "Über den ersten reinen Fall eines Menschen mit völligem, isoliertem Verlust der Mehrfahrigkeit (Concerning the First Clear Case of a Person with Complete Isolated Loss of Attentive Capacity)," *Archiv für die Gesamte Psychologie,* LXXXI (1931), 257-384.

(14) *Op. cit.* (9). Pp. 585-588.

(15) Wiggers, Carl J. "The Heart," *Scientific American* (May, 1957), 75.

(16) *Op. cit.* (12). Pp. 184-185.

(17) Cowdry, E. V. *Problems of Aging.* Baltimore: The Williams and Wilkins Company, 1939. Pp. 547-548.

(18) Hovland, Carl I. "Human Learning and Retention," in *Handbook of Experimental Psychology.* Ed., S. S. Stevens. New York: John Wiley & Sons, Inc., 1951. Pp. 632-633.

(19) Freud, Sigmund. "Psychopathology of Everyday Life," in *The Basic*

Writings of Sigmund Freud. Tr. & ed., A. A. Brill. New York: The
Modern Library, 1938. P. 52.

(20) Freud, Sigmund. *A General Introduction to Psychoanalysis.* Tr., Joan
Riviere. Garden City, N. Y.: Garden City Publishing Company, 1943.
P. 50.

(21) *Ibid.* Pp. 52-53.

(22) *Ibid.* P. 39.

(23) Bach, George R. "Some Diadic Functions of Childhood Memories,"
Journal of Psychology, XXXIII (1952), 87-98.

(24) Layton, E. T. "The Persistence of Learning in Elementary Algebra,"
Journal of Educational Psychology, XXIII (1932), 46-55.

(25) Greene, E. B. "The Retention of Information Learned in College
Courses," *Journal of Educational Research,* XXIV (1931), 262-273.

(26) Watson, R. I. "An Experimental Study of the Permanence of Course
Material in Introductory Psychology," *Archives of Psychology,* No. 225
(1938), 64.

(27) Garrett, Henry E. *Great Experiments in Psychology.* New York: Century
Publishing Company, 1930. Pp. 62-63.

(28) Davis, R. A., and Moore, C. C. "Methods of Measuring Retention,"
Journal of General Psychology, XII (1935), 144-155. Or see R. A
Davis. *Psychology of Learning.* New York: McGraw-Hill Publishing
Company, Inc., 1935. Pp. 212, 213.

(29) Smith, Madorah E. "Childhood Memories Compared with Those of
Adult Life," *Journal of Genetic Psychology,* LXXX (1952), 151-182.

(30) Woodworth, R. S. *Psychology.* 3rd ed. New York: Henry Holt and
Company, 1934. Pp. 275-280.

(31) Swift, E. J. "Memory of Skillful Movements," *Psychological Bulletin,*
III (1906), 185-187.

(32) Burri, C. "The Influence of an Audience upon Recall," *Journal of Educational Psychology,* XXII (1931), 683-690.

(33) Montague, Ernest K. "The Role of Anxiety in Serial Rote Learning,"
Journal of Experimental Psychology, XLV (1953), 91-96.

(34) Müller, G. E., and Pilzecker, A. "Retroactive Inhibition," Experimentelle
Beiträge zur Lehre vom Gedachtnis, *Zeitschrift für Psychologie,* Erbgd.
I (1900), 344, 355.

(35) McGeoch, John A. "The Influence of Four Different Interpolated Activities upon Retention," *Journal of Experimental Psychology,* XIV
(1931), 400-413.

(36) *Ibid.*

(37) Waters, R. H., and Peel, Z. E. "Similarity in the Form of Original and
Interpolated Learning and Retroactive Inhibition," *American Journal
of Psychology,* XLVII (1935), 477-481.

(38) Jenkins, J. G., and Dallenbach, K. M. "Obliviscence during Sleep and
Waking," *American Journal of Psychology,* XXXV (1924), 605-612.

(39) Whitely, P. I., and Blankenship, A. B. "The Influence of Certain Conditions Prior to Learning upon Subsequent Recall," *Journal of Experimental Psychology,* XIX (1936), 496-504.

Chapter V:

(1) Mathieu, J. "Erziehung zum exakten optischen Auffassen und Einprägen nach der Poppelreuterschen psychokritischen Methodik (Training toward Exact Optical Comprehension and Impression by the Poppelreuter Psychocritical Method)," *Zeitschrift für Angewandte Psychologie und Psychologische Sammelforschung,* XLI (1932), 366-422.

(2) Dunlap, Knight. "A Revision of the Fundamental Law of Habit Formation," *Science,* LXVII (1928), 360-362. Also: "The Technique of Negative Practice," *American Journal of Psychology,* LV (1942), 270-273.

(3) Kellogg, W. N., and White, R. E. "A Maze Test of Dunlap's Theory of Learning," *Journal of Comparative Psychology,* XIX (1935), 119-148.

(4) Tilton, J. W. *An Educational Psychology of Learning.* New York: The Macmillan Company, 1951. P. 102.

(5) Droba, D. D. "Effect of Printed Information on Memory for Pictures," *Museum News,* VII (1929), No. 5.

(6) Leible, Otto. "Zur Psychologie der Aussage (The Psychology of Testimony)," *Zeitschrift für die Gesamte Kriminalistische Wissenschaft und Praxis,* IX (1935), 273-276.

(7) Hayes, S. P. "The Memory of Blind Children," *Teachers' Forum (Blind),* VIII (1936), I—55-59 and II—71-77.

(8) Thisted, M. N., and Remmers, Hermann H. "The Effect of Temporal Set on Learning," *Journal of Applied Psychology,* XVI (1932), 257-268.

(9) Warden, C. J. "The Factor of Movement in the Presentation of Rote Memory Material," *American Journal of Psychology,* XXXVII (1926), 257-260.

(10) Hennig, R. "Die Zahl der datierbaren Erinnerungen eines Menschen leben (The Number of Datable Memories in a Human Life)," *Zeitschrift für Psychologie,* CXL (1937), 330-356.

(11) Murphy, G. *Personality.* New York: Harper and Brothers, 1947. P. 373.

(12) Miller, George. "Remember Seven Items," *Science News Letter* (December 31, 1955), 422.

Chapter VI:

(1) Ruch, F. *Psychology and Life.* New York: Scott, Foresman and Compan 1953. P. 305.

(2) Bartlett, F. C. *Remembering.* London: Cambridge University Press, 1932. Pp. 61, 110-112.

(3) Gates, Arthur I. "Recitation as a Factor in Memorizing," *Archives of Psychology,* VII (1917), No. 40.

(4) Sherman, Stuart P. "Franklin," in *The Cambridge History of American Literature.* New York: The Macmillan Company, 1933. Vol. I, pp. 108-109

(5) Piéron, H. "Recherches experimentales sur les phénoménes de mémoire," Année Psychologique, XIX (1913), 91-193.

(6) Zeigarnik, B. "Das Behalten erledigter und unerledigter Handlungen," Psychologische Forschungen, IX (1927), 1-85.

(7) Lewin, Kurt. "Untersuchungen zur Handlungs und Affektpsychologie (Investigations on the Psychology of Action and Emotion)": III, Zei-garnik, B., "Das Behalten erledigter und unerledigter Handlungen (The Memory of Completed and Uncompleted Actions)," Psychologische Forschungen, IX (1927), 1-85.

(8) Op. cit. (5). Pp. 62-63.

(9) Maity, H. P. "Diurnal Course of Efficiency," Indian Journal of Psychology, IV (1929), 127-133.

(10) Garrett, Henry E. Great Experiments in Psychology. New York: The Century Company, 1930. Pp. 57-58.

Chapter VII:

(1) Bacon, Francis. Philosophical Works. Ed., John M. Robertson. London: George Routledge and Sons, Ltd., 1905. P. 519.

(2) Wells, H. G. The Outline of History. Garden City, N. Y.: Garden City Publishing Company, 1920. P. 361.

(3) Woodworth, Robert S. Experimental Psychology. New York: Henry Holt and Company, 1938. P. 10.

Chapter VIII:

(1) Woodworth, Robert S. Psychology. 3rd ed. New York: Henry Holt and Company, 1934. P. 275.

(2) Hovland, Carl I. "Human Learning and Retention," in Handbook of Experimental Psychology. Ed., S. S. Stevens. New York: John Wiley & Sons, Inc., 1951. Pp. 640-641.

(3) Woodworth, R. S. Experimental Psychology. New York: Henry Holt and Company, 1938. P. 223.